LifERS'

LEARN THE TRUTH AT THE EXPENSE OF OUR SORROW

WRITTEN AND PHOTOGRAPHED BY
RICHARD WORMSER

JULIAN MESSNER

For my mother and for Annie

Acknowledgments

The author is deeply grateful to the Lifers' Group of East Jersey State Prison, whose trust made this book possible.

The author would like to thank Superintendent Patrick Arvonio, the staff of East Jersey State Prison, the New Jersey Department of Corrections and especially Lieutenant Alan August, for their cooperation.

Copyright © 1991 by Richard Wormser
All rights reserved including the right of reproduction in whole or in part in any form.
Published by Julian Messner, a division of Silver Burdett Press, Inc., Simon & Schuster, Inc.
Prentice Hall Bldg., Englewood Cliffs, NJ 07632

JULIAN MESSNER and colophon are trademarks of Simon & Schuster, Inc.
Design by Greg Wozney
Manufactured in the United States of America
Lib. ed. 10 9 8 7 6 5 4 3 2 1
paper ed. 10 9 8 7 6 5 4 3 2 1

Library of Congress Cataloging-in-Publication Data

Wormser, Richard.
   Lifers : learn the truth at the expense of our sorrow / by Richard
Wormser.
      p.   cm.
   Includes index.
   1. Prisoners—New Jersey—Biography.   2. East Jersey State Prison.
Lifers' Group—Biography.   3. Life imprisonment—New Jersey—Case
studies.   4. Juvenile delinquency—New Jersey—Prevention—Case
studies.   I. Title.
HV9468.W67   1991
365'.6'092274938—dc20
   [B]   90-19237
                                                                  CIP
                                                                  AC

ISBN: 0-671-72548-3 (LSB)
ISBN: 0-671-72549-1 (pbk.)

LIFERS' GROUP
SCARED STRAIGHT PROJECT
LOCK BAG R — RAHWAY, NEW JERSEY 07065

Harvey George - PRESIDENT   Maxwell Melvins - VICE PRESIDENT
Qahhar Saahir - TREASURER   Tariq Commander - SECRETARY
          Willie Allen - EXECUTIVE VICE PRESIDENT
        Hakeem Shakoor - EXECUTIVE VICE PRESIDENT
****

July 18, 1990

Dear Young Friends;

     We the members of the Lifers' Group "Scared Straight Program",
would like for you to know a few important facts, number one you
have the power of CHOICE.

     This book will tell you about our dreams, our hopes, our
failures, our despair, and most of all about the consequences of bad
choices. When we agreed to share our lives with you, many of us
were not ready for the pain and agony that reviewing a life of bad
choices could create. I don't think anyone should have to relive
there mistakes twice in one life. In many of our minds we would
like to live in amnesia of our bad choices, and for those of us who
have repeatedly fell into this pit of hell, it would seem that
amnesia is just what we had. But with counseling and the desire not
to see any more of our lives or any one elses lives wasted in this
man made hell hole, we bring to you all the reasons why you should
seek out the right choices in life.

     When you read this book, don't make the mistake of thinking
that anyone involved in this book is happy about anything that has
taken place in their lives. There is one thing that this book can
not capture, and that is mental and inner suffering that goes on
each second, minute, hour, day, week, and year that past by. There
is no true friendship or love in this hell, and the only one that
might stand by you will be your mother, IF you have been a decent
person to her. Many parents will give up on you when you have
repeatedly ignored their warnings, and will not spend the rest of
their lives coming to a prison. So it is our deepest desire that
when you read this, you will be able to understand why, this is not
the place for you or any human being. But if you are not able to
make the right choices, society will make a choice for you.

                         Sincerely Your Choice

                         Mr. Harvey George
                         Lifers' Group President
                         "SCARED STRAIGHT PROJECT"

"HELPING TO SAVE TOMORROW'S MINDS FROM CRIME TODAY"

Juvenile Project	Hotline	Executive Staff
(201) 574-2510	(201) 574-2107	(201) 574-3375

And how much youth lay uselessly buried behind these walls, what mighty powers were wasted here in vain? After all, one must tell the whole truth. These men were exceptional men. Perhaps they were the most gifted. Their mighty energies were vainly wasted, wasted abnormally, unjustly, hopelessly. And who was to blame, whose fault was it?

That's just it, who was to blame?

Feodor Dostoyevsky,
THE HOUSE OF THE DEAD.

TABLE OF CONTENTS

The home of the Juvenile Awareness Program—East Jersey State Prison, Rahway, NJ.

SOME GRIM STATISTICS
PREFACE

There are more than 1 million men and women in prison throughout America. Six hundred thousand are in state institutions, 100,000 in federal penitentiaries, and 350,000 in local jails. Every year 10 million people are arrested and almost as many are released.

The average length of a prison sentence is seven years. Forty-four percent of those who are released return. Every year approximately 1,500 men, women, and teenagers die while incarcerated. Most kill themselves, while others are executed or die from disease or violence.

The juvenile statistics are equally grim. Last year almost 1.5 million young people under eighteen were arrested. Six hundred thousand of them were arrested for crimes that would have been criminal offenses had they been adults. More than 100,000 juveniles are presently in custody. Fifty-two percent of all juveniles in custody are white, 34 percent black, and 12 percent Hispanic. Seventy-nine percent of the incarcerated youth are male and 21 percent female. Almost 40 percent of the crimes committed by juveniles in state institutions were for violent offenses. More than 60 percent used drugs and almost 40 percent were under the influence of drugs when they committed their crimes. Seven out of every ten did not live with their families and over half grew up in a single-parent home. Almost half had been arrested five times or more and 20 percent ten times or more. And more than half had a family member that had been in prison at some time, usually the father.

Prisons have existed in America for more than two hundred years. They were introduced by the Quakers who, in the late eighteenth century, believed prison was a humane way to treat criminals. Prior to the Quakers, prisons in both the American colonies and Europe were used mainly to incarcerate persons of rank and importance or persons who were considered to be a danger to the state. Captured kings, queens, and nobles were imprisoned, as were religious heretics and thinkers whose ideas were considered to be offensive to public morality. Common criminals—thieves, murderers, and pickpockets—were hanged. Those who committed lesser crimes were mutilated, branded, flogged, or locked in stocks. All punishment was carried out in public and treated as a spectacle, much like a sporting event is today.

The American Quakers saw prison as a means of saving the criminal's soul and changing him. Their method was to lock a prisoner in solitary confinement for long periods of time with only a Bible and a candle, and deny him any human contact. The theory was that he would reflect upon his crimes, repent, and thus be saved. In practice, prisoners went mad or killed themselves because they could not stand the isolation.

In the nineteenth century, new philosophies flourished concerning prisons. In 1870 Zebulan Brockaway, then warden of the Detroit House of Correction, proclaimed in a burst of enthusiasm: "Let prisons and prison systems be lighted by the law of love! Let us leave, for the present, the thought of inflicting punishment upon prisoners to satisfy so-called justice and turn toward the reformation of prisoners." For almost one hundred years, prisons were considered places where criminals could be reformed, or rehabilitated. The reality failed to match the ideal. The majority of people sent to prison were not rehabilitated and often came out more determined and skillful criminals.

Today most prisons in America are little more than "warehouses" in which people considered to be dangerous to society are kept for a period of time. Prisons are regarded as places of punishment where rehabilitation is the exception, not the rule. If once prison was considered to be an effective deterrent to crime, today the results are less certain. According to the Justice Department, out of every 100 major crimes committed in the United States, only 50 are reported to police. Twelve out of the 50 people are arrested, 6 convicted, and only 1.5 go to jail. The cost of keeping a man in prison averages about $30,000 a year. Many prisoners say that if they had been able to earn that much money on the outside, they wouldn't have come to prison in the first place.

If there is relatively little success in getting people off the prison track once they are on it, a huge amount of energy and effort is being spent to keep young people out of prison. Every year millions of adolescents throughout America are involved in criminal offenses that could lead them to prison— car theft, breaking and entering, purse snatching, and drug dealing. In addition, many juveniles commit acts that often lead to crime, such as malicious mischief, drug and alcohol abuse, dropping out of school, and running away from home. About 13 percent of all juvenile offenses are crimes against persons.

While many agencies try to keep young people out of prison, their counselors often struggle to overcome the attraction of the streets with their illusionary promises of easy money, pleasure, and excitement. Troubled teenagers some-times "tune out" adults whose experiences and background are different from their own, feeling that they lack the author-ity and understanding to speak to them about their lives.

The men you will meet in this book are able to speak with authority when it comes to crime. They are "lifers"—men in prison who are serving life terms at East Jersey State Prison in Rahway, New Jersey. Some have killed or been in-volved in killings. Many have used or sold drugs, robbed houses, or stolen cars. Most of them will spend between fifteen and twenty years in prison before they are released. A few may never be released. Having lived most of their lives in prison, they will die in prison. Yet all of them use the failures in their own lives to help young people avoid the same mis-takes they made.

In 1975 four lifers who were part of an organization known as the Lifers' Group at East Jersey State Prison re-ceived permission to start a program to help keep troubled teenagers out of jail. The program, known as the Juvenile Awareness Program, was an almost instant success. It became famous throughout the world when a documentary film on the program called *Scared Straight* was shown on television. The film emphasized the dramatic techniques the lifers used to make teenagers aware of the brutality of prison life. The film showed tough, seemingly hardened convicts screaming and cursing at a group of troubled young people, describing in highly-graphic language prison life in all its violence. But their goal was not simply to scare young people, but to make them aware that their delinquent behavior could lead them to prison. To achieve this goal, many of the lifers began to work with the young people on a one-on-one basis to help them straighten out their troubled lives.

Since the program began, the lifers have spoken to 35,000 young people directly and reached millions more through the film and other channels of communication. Every year some 2,500 new teenagers come into the program. And as the lifers and young people face each other, each can see an image of themselves in the other's face. In the faces of the prisoners, young people can see what they will be like in thirty years should they come to prison. In the faces of the young people, the lifers see the image of their own lost youth. To many of them the program has given them a chance to redeem their own lives by saving the lives of others. Their motto expresses this feeling. "Most of us are here because we took a life. Now we have a chance to give a life back."

When the gate slams shut, you've entered "the belly of the beast."

A NEW FISH

CHAPTER 1

From a distance, Billy could see the ninety-year-old prison shaped like a steel and stone octopus. A huge brick dome squatted in the center of four equally spaced brick buildings that extended from it like tentacles. A thirty-foot concrete wall topped with towers containing armed guards surrounded one part of the prison; the other was surrounded by fences trimmed with spiral rolls of barbed wire that seemed like the teeth of a ferocious shark. Behind the fences, small groups of men played basketball. Later Billy would learn they were kept in solitary confinement and allowed out of their cells one hour a day for recreation. The van in which Billy and nine other prisoners were riding, their legs shackled in irons, their wrists handcuffed, turned off the highway and onto the prison grounds.

Billy had finally made it to the big time. He and his partner had held up a convenience store. As Billy took the money out of the cash register, the clerk made a sudden move and his partner shot the man through the heart. Even though Billy didn't carry a weapon, he was still sentenced to life in prison for the killing. "The hand of one is the hand of all," the judge had told him as he delivered the sentence. "Being part of a crime in which someone is killed makes you as guilty as if you had pulled the trigger yourself." Billy was eighteen years old and would have to spend at least twenty-five years in prison before he would be eligible for parole.

The van headed toward the huge steel receiving gate in the rear of the prison. Between the road and the prison lay a small pond where hundreds of gray and white sea gulls and brown and gray geese sat side by side. Billy wondered why birds of different species didn't fight each other over territory. Gulls were tough, he thought. He had seen them peck each other in the sky. But geese could be nasty, too. Maybe each knew that the other guy was as tough as he was. Maybe they just didn't care.

The van stopped in a large patch of sunlight in front of the steel gate. The gate opened with a groan and the van entered inside and was swallowed up in darkness. The gate slammed closed with a bang. Billy had entered inside what a prisoner once called "the belly of the beast." Once the gate shut behind him, Billy and the other prisoners stepped down from the van and the guards unfastened their irons and hand-cuffs. Now that they were in prison, they were "free."

The corrections officers escorted Billy and the others into the main building. First he was stripped-searched, standing naked as officers thoroughly examined his body to make sure that he wasn't smuggling narcotics or a weapon into the prison. Despite the fact that he had grown up in jails, Billy always felt a deep sense of shame and humiliation at this intimate invasion of his body. Then he was photographed. His number, 92603, was placed under his chin. As far as prison authorities were concerned, Billy's number was his official name. The strobe light flashed three times in succession, momentarily blinding Billy. The picture would be laminated on his ID Card, which he would have to carry with him at all times. Without it, he could not receive mail, go to the commissary, or receive a visitor. Without his card, Billy would be a nonperson.

In the storeroom, Billy was handed the basic supplies

A prisoner's number is his name—he must carry it on an ID card.

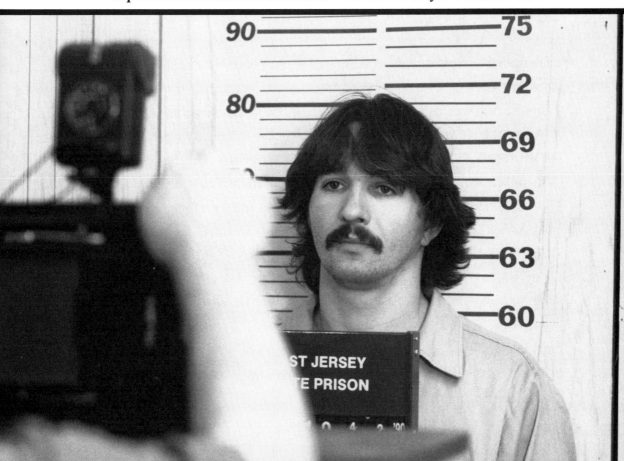

for prison life—a plastic bucket, a towel, a toothbrush, toothpaste, a comb, a bar of soap, sheets, pillowcases, blankets, two pair of pants, two shirts, socks, work boots, and toilet paper. As he stuffed his supplies into his bucket, he could hear men refer to him as the "new fish"—a new prisoner.

When he entered the heart of the prison, Billy thought he was hallucinating. A mass movement was on and hundreds of men flowed through the prison, traveling back and forth from their wings to work or recreation, from the yard to the wings, from classroom to classroom. The cycle of the movement seemed synchronized to the rhythm of bells and distorted voices over the public address system. As Billy passed by these moving lines, men looked at him. He met their eyes directly. He knew they were testing him. They wanted to see if he was a man or a "punk." Would he defend himself if challenged or would he need someone to protect him? In a juvenile detention center where he had once been incarcerated for stealing cars, a prisoner had swaggered over and demanded Billy hand over his cigarettes to him. Billy had smashed him with a lock wrapped in a sock and earned himself a reputation as someone to be respected. But a maximum security prison was far more intense than a juvenile detention center. It was like the crater of a sleeping volcano. On the surface, everything seemed calm. Most officers were polite, if distant. Prisoners dressed in street clothes rather than prison uniforms. They had personal possessions. Men watched television and lounged in their cells or played basketball in the yard and gym. Yet the potential for violence was lurking everywhere and in everyone. It could erupt at any moment without warning, and could strike anyone for any reason or for no reason at all. Billy knew that sooner or later he would have to "make his bones" and fight. It might be over cigarettes, food, money, sex, clothing, a postage stamp, or nothing at all. He only hoped it would be on his own ground and on his own terms. He hoped he would not have to kill anyone—and that he himself would not be killed. He would have to make a "shank" to protect himself. He would steal a spoon from the mess hall, sharpen its handle to a point by grinding it on the concrete floor of his cell, wrap it in tape, and hide it behind the sink in his cell, to use when that moment of truth arrived.

"Open!"

The iron gate to Four Wing slid open and Billy and the corrections officer passed through. Once they were inside, the gate slid shut with a crash and Billy gave a little start. They climbed two flights of stairs to the third tier known as "four-up" (Four Wing, upper tier) and then through another gate and down a corridor. Billy passed a long row of cells. Some were dark and empty. In others, men watched television, read, slept, or stood in the entrance. Some cells had makeshift curtains hung up over the bars so that the man inside could sleep. A man, naked from the waist up, washed his clothes in a sink and Billy could see a deep scar from a knife wound across his lower back. Another man, with a face much older than his years, with long gray and black hair tied in a pony tail, a long gray beard knotted at the end, and clear blue eyes, looked up from his ironing and watched Billy with a blank expression as he passed. Billy wondered if that's how he would look at the end of his term. As Billy reached the end of a long corridor, a huge, muscular man, bald, wearing a headband and dressed in shorts and a sleeveless jersey, stepped out of his cell and looked directly at Billy with contempt. Their eyes met and Billy looked away. He cursed himself for showing weakness.

"Open 32!"

The officer yelled out and the gate of Billy's cell opened. It was dark and Billy could only get a sense of its size. But as soon as he stepped inside, he felt sick to his stomach. The cell was so small that Billy could stand in the middle of the room and easily touch the opposite walls if he stretched out his arms. Four feet wide by six feet long. He turned on the light. A bed with a rolled-up mattress was wedged against one wall, a dresser against the other, with a narrow space between them that was barely wide enough for a man to walk through. In the back of the room was the toilet and a cold-water sink. Billy switched off his light and sat on his bed in the dark as the cell door closed behind him.

For an hour, Billy sat in his cell without moving, listening to the noises around him: bells going off, gates rumbling open and slamming shut, men talking and shouting, announcements blasting over the public address system. Twenty-five years, he thought. How many weeks was that? He began to calculate the number of weeks, days, hours, minutes, and seconds that he would have to spend in prison before he could even be considered for parole: 1,300 weeks. 9,100 days. 218,400 hours. 13,104,000 minutes. 786,240,000 seconds. Could he do the time? How could he do it? How could anyone live in a cell for almost a billion seconds of his life? He was seized by a deep feeling of numbness and despair. He thought of killing himself; perhaps everyone would be better off if he was dead. He had always felt himself to be worthless and no good to anyone. He felt he could not survive prison life, that he would be killed or kill himself long before his sentence was up. But until then, he vowed to do things his own way. He would not take any orders he didn't want to take, or put up with anything he didn't want to put up with. He would make himself a weapon and if he was killed in a fight, so much the better. He could not imagine watching his youth and most of his adult life pass away in prison. Death was better than that. As Billy's gloom deepened, the bell rang sounding the midday count. Throughout the prison, every single inmate was ac-

Some cells are so small that a prisoner can stand in the middle and touch opposite walls.

counted for by the corrections officers. Then, suddenly, the gate to Billy's cell slid open. It was lunchtime for Four Wing.

The line of men moved rapidly toward the mess hall, like a river rushing to the sea. As Billy approached the dining room, he could hear the low roar of voices. Inside six hundred men were eating or waiting on line to be served. As soon as he entered, Billy began to look around. Where should he sit? With whom could he share a table? Whom could he talk to? Whom could he trust? A sea of faces was before him. Faces of old men and young men, black and white and Hispanic. Angry faces and faces filled with despair. Faces of defeat and resignation mixed occasionally with faces of determination and pride. Men with wild looks and madness in their eyes and men with blank, dead eyes, burned out from having been in prison too long. Billy moved forward to be served, avoiding all eye contact, walking with a swagger, pretending to be tough, hiding the fear within him, knowing that even though no one looked directly at him, he was being watched and judged by the men who surrounded him.

For the first two weeks in prison, Billy attended an orientation program that introduced him to the rules of the prison and the way it operated. Members of the staff and inmate group leaders instructed him about the various programs available and what would be expected of him. He learned about work assignments, educational opportunities, legal and medical assistance, mailroom procedures, commissary privileges, recreation and religious services, social services, therapeutic programs, and a variety of different prisoners' groups and committees. He was handed a 125-page manual in which every rule and pertinent piece of information about prison life was listed and explained. It included the 77 offenses for which he could be punished, the conditions for parole, security, marriages, packages, visits, telephone calls, reading material, and how he might reduce his sentence. Billy read this last part first. Once orientation ended, he merged into the daily rhythm of prison life.

The routine that Billy followed in prison the first day would be the pattern for the next twenty-five years of his life, with only minor variations. At 6:20 A.M. Billy will be awakened by a loud ring of a bell and counted. At 6:45 he will go out to the yard to box or lift weights. At 7:15 he will eat breakfast, which usually consists of cereal, juice, two pieces of toast, a carton of milk, and coffee. Occasionally, he will receive eggs. After breakfast, he will return to his wing. If he has a job, he will move to work at 8:00.

If Billy chooses not to work, he can go to the recreation hall or the yard at 8:20 and play basketball. Or he can hang out in his wing and play cards. Or he can sit in his cell, watch television, and become one of the hundreds of men in prison whose total existence revolves around soap operas, basketball, and meals.

At 10 A.M. Billy will return from recreation and take a shower. If he works in a shop, he will return to his wing at 11:15. At 11:30 he will be counted for the second time that day. Within the next hour, he will go to lunch, then return to his cell. At 12:50 P.M. workers will be called out again, followed by recreation a half-hour later. At 2:20 all wings will be secured and another count taken. At 3:20 the shop workers will return to their wings and at 3:30 the fourth count of the day will be taken. At 4:00 boxers and weight lifters will go out to the yard and the first shift of dinner begins. Men will take showers in the late afternoon. Between 5:45 and 6:00 another count will be taken.

At 6 o'clock recreation will begin and will last through most of the evening. Every Tuesday evening, between the hours of 6:00 and 8:00, Billy will be allowed to go to the commissary to buy candy bars, soap, toothpaste, detergent, and more than one hundred items of household goods for his personal use. By 9:15 the final count of the day will be taken and the men will be locked up in their wings for the night. Inside his cell, Billy can watch television, read, write letters, think, or stare up at the ceiling all night until he is ready to sleep. Another day has ended. Only 9,099 to go.

"Got a cigarette?" Billy heard a voice behind him and turned around. Behind him was an older prisoner who looked like a hermit. Billy gave him a cigarette. The older man began to talk with him, but Billy, while politely responding, kept his distance. In prison the rule is every man for himself. There is no one you can really trust, no one you can confide in. Nobody asks you your crime and nobody tells you theirs. Any man who boasts of what he did or how much money he made on the street is generally regarded with suspicion as either a fool or a liar—or both. The man who offers you friendship may be secretly planning to rob or assault you or make you his servant or slave. Alliances are sometimes formed for mutual protection. Race and religion bring some men together. A few form friendships based solely on mutual interests and respect. But most of the time, men inside have "associates," rather then friends.

In the fifth month after his arrival, Billy was initiated

into one of the grim realities of prison life. One morning, as he was eating breakfast, a fellow convict quietly slid up behind him, rested his left hand on Billy's shoulder, and with the grace of a dancer, leaned over him and savagely slashed the throat of the man seated opposite Billy. The wounded man screamed and grabbed his throat. Blood spurted onto the table and over Billy's breakfast. Billy's first thought was to pretend it didn't happen. The basic law of survival in prison is to mind your own business. Billy deliberately did not turn around to see who had done the slashing. He heard the riot bell ring and saw officers wearing helmets and carrying clubs pour into the dining room and grab the assailant as he fled. Billy sat motionless as the wounded man cried out for help and held his neck to contain the bleeding. The wound, despite its bloody appearance, was superficial. The injured prisoner was taken to the hospital, while his attacker was locked in solitary confinement. Billy looked at the blood-soaked scrambled eggs on his plate and for a moment fantasized that they were covered with ketchup. Then he felt dizzy and sick to his stomach. Later on he would learn to harden himself to violence so that in similar situations he would be able to act as if nothing had happened.

Billy's first fight erupted several months later over a chair in the schoolroom where he was taking courses to finish his high school education. The classroom was crowded and a prisoner had put his books on the last vacant chair in the room. Billy politely asked him to remove them so that he could sit down. The man said nothing but just looked at him. Billy removed the books, carefully placed them on the floor, and took the chair to sit in. Without warning, the man grabbed the chair from under Billy, throwing him violently to the floor. The anger that had been building inside of Billy since he entered prison erupted and he tore into the man with such violence that it took four corrections officers to pull them apart. The man had to be taken to the hospital with a broken nose and jaw. Billy was sent to "the hole"—solitary confinement—for ten days, a relatively mild sentence because he did not start the fight.

For twenty-three hours of every day, Billy was locked in his cell. The first day, he enjoyed the solitude. Meals were brought to his cell three times a day. He had books to read. He could write. He was proud to have earned himself a reputation as a tough guy for beating up a man who disrespected him. In prison that was what manhood was all about. But he was concerned that the man he injured might seek revenge and was relieved to learn through the grapevine that the prison authorities had shipped the man to another prison. True, Billy was not allowed visits and he missed seeing his family. He was not allowed to use the commissary. There was no one he could talk with while he was in his cell. There was no television for him to look at. He was not allowed into the yard. The only thing that broke the monotony was the shower he was permitted to take every three days.

By the third day, the isolation began to take its toll on Billy. He became bored with reading and found he had nothing to write about. He lay on his bed and stared at the ceiling and thought of good times he had enjoyed in the past, the girls he had known, his family and friends, meals he had eaten, parties he had gone to, the times he had gotten high and drunk. He slept often, for short periods of time, like a cat napping. In

Isolation takes its toll inside a windowless cell.

his windowless cell, day merged with night and each tedious minute dragged by as if it were an hour. He began to tire of everything, mostly of himself and the dead-end life that had led him into prison. He began to think of what he could do with himself in prison. There must be something, he thought. There must be something that could save his life from becoming a total loss. But what could he accomplish inside prison? And how? He knew other men did it. What was their secret? He vowed that once released from solitary, he would find out.

The Lifers' Executive Board paints its wishes on the wall (from left to right: Tariq Commander, Qahhar Saahir, Hakeem Shakoor, Harvey George, Raashid Ali)

CHAPTER 2

Life! To hear a judge pronounce those words as he sentences a man to prison pulls the earth from under his feet. "It couldn't have been me the judge was talking about," Kevin Finney remembered thinking. "There was no one else in the court, but it couldn't have been me." Another prisoner recalled: "My heart stopped when he said it. I was dizzy and wanted to throw up." And a third said: "The only thing he could have said that was worse than 'life' was 'death,' and it would have been kinder for him to have said it."

In the state of New Jersey, as well as many other states, a minimum sentence of life in prison must be given to any person who is convicted of deliberately killing another person. Under certain conditions, the death penalty can also be imposed, especially if the crime is considered by the judge or jury to be especially cruel or violent. In New Jersey the homicides that usually result in life sentences include impulsive killings and homicides committed in the act of a felony such as robbery.

At East Jersey State Prison, more commonly known by its former name of Rahway Prison, some 300 men out of the 2,200 incarcerated there are serving life terms or long-term sentences. While it is commonly believed that only those who commit murder receive life sentences, in reality some lifers have never personally committed a violent crime in their lives. Their misfortune was to have been present when a violent crime was committed or in some way contributed to it. The youth sitting in the car while his friend shoots and kills a store owner can be equally guilty in the eyes of the law, even though he may not have even known that his friend had a gun. There are other men serving life terms for being habitual offenders. These men may never have injured anyone, but because they have committed more than two felonies they can be sentenced to life in prison under the present law. "You don't have to rap three times on the jail house door before they let you in," lifer Harvey George notes. "Just be in the wrong place at the wrong time once, and the gate will swing wide open for you."

On the other hand, many lifers have killed people. They have killed in a variety of circumstances for a variety of reasons. Some killed in a moment of rage and passion and others killed for hire. Some have killed for revenge, while a few are psychopathic killers. Many have killed during the course of a robbery—often committed to get money for drugs. And usually the person who killed was high during the commission of his crime. As Superintendent Patrick Arvonio points out, "I would say that almost seventy percent of the men in here are here because of drug involvement, either as a dealer or user or both."

In their youth, many lifers saw crime as a natural way of life for them. Superintendent Arvonio notes that "when the norm is criminal activity, it's hard to turn people around. It's as hard to get some people to go straight as it is for some people to go crooked." King Webster, a lifer and now a licensed minister, confirms that observation. "I was born into that life style. My life style was drug-dealing, pimping. For others it was stickup or bank robbery. That was the norm. Those who were doing it were our role models. In another life style, I might have been a lawyer or preacher as I am today."

For many men in prison, their life of crime began in childhood. Stealing and playing hooky before they were ten. Alcohol or drugs before they were thirteen. Arrested for breaking and entering and car theft before they were fifteen. Growing up in detention homes and reform schools, where they learned to become more skillful criminals.

For Akbar Harris, a life of serious crime began at age thirteen when he got his hands on a gun. "We used to steal cars from a lot in which the driver would leave the key in the ignition. When we got the gun, we said 'to hell with sneaking in, let's go over there and stick it in his face and get the car what we want.' We used to brag about it, how we stuck the gun in a guy's face and he started crying like a baby, 'please please, don't shoot me' and this and that and we went in and tied him up and took all his money and picked out the car we wanted."

Michael Thompson was thirteen years old the first time he was picked up by the police for stealing a battery out of a car. It happened to be a police car. An honor student in school whose teachers told him he was college material, Michael found life on the streets more appealing than the university. Instead of books, he carried a sawed-off shotgun. By the time he reached fifteen, he was involved in a shootout with the police. A holdup went bad and Michael and his two companions tried to escape the police in a high-speed chase.

"Before I knew it," Michael recalled, "the police was on top of me shooting. I had a sawed-off shotgun, but I never had the chance to shoot back. I was running so fast because I heard something jingling and I thought it was police right behind me. It was coins in my pocket. I tried to get to the lake in the park and thought I could swim to the other side. But it wasn't deep enough and they caught me. They took me out, threw me on the ground, and started stomping me. I don't know why I did this but I started laughing. The cop said later on, 'you was really lucky. I just missed shooting you.' I was sarcastic. I said: 'Maybe you wasn't such a good shot.' "

Joey Mackiewicz was a white kid who grew up in the ghettos of Newark. "I used to run with integrated gangs robbing people and beating up other gangs. My father abandoned us and my mother couldn't work. That's the cards I was dealt. I didn't know how to handle them. There was nobody there to teach me how to handle them. As a teenager, me and my buddies could make ninety thousand dollars from stealing coats in warehouses. We spent it faster than we made it. Cars, booze, women. My mother seen these things. She knew something was wrong. How's she gonna handle a kid like me? What's she going to say to me when I'm decked out in nice new pants, coats and things, and I hand her a couple hundred one day, couple hundred the next? What's she going to say when she has to eat mush—powdered milk and white bread—because she's so poor, when rats are running around the house at night? She's hurting inside. She knew I was doing the wrong thing. She wanted something better for me.

Almost seventy percent of the men in this prison have had some drug involvement. Chris is one.

"It's not that I wanted to be a criminal. I wanted to do the right thing. I wanted help. I tried to get into the service. When they turned me away, it rocked my whole life. When I had to leave the Job Corps, that rocked my world. It seemed that everytime I tried to do the right thing, something knocked me back down. It was as if somebody were saying, 'yeah, you don't belong here. Get back down in the ghetto where you belong.'"

By the time he was eighteen, Qahhar Saahir was already deep into a life of crime. "I wanted money, lots of money and I didn't want to work for it. When I went out to rob a store or a check-cashing place, and I got over, it also gave me a natural high which I liked. In my mind, I played against the odds and I beat them. I'm not thinking that I'm going to kill somebody. I'm only thinking that I want money in my pocket. I don't want to work for it even though I had jobs working as an auto mechanic and at a youth center. I just wanted money. I had a thing for money. And after I made money, after I went out and robbed and put fear in people by holding a gun to their head, I went to the gambling hall and lost it all. I remember I seen a house that one of my friends had bought. He was about sixteen. He bought a one-family house for thirty-five thousand dollars. I was intrigued by this. I said to myself 'before I'm eighteen, I'm going to have one.' I knew I could get the money if I went out and robbed. I got the money, but instead, I went to the gambling house and lost it all. I didn't care. I could always go out and get more. It didn't matter who I stuck up . . . dope dealers, so-called tough guys, store owners. Me and my crew were the bullies out there. In order to sell any drugs in our neighborhood, you had to pay us. Otherwise we'd beat you up, take your drugs and your money. I wanted to be that gangster like in the James Cagney movies."

The image of the gangster also appealed to Bilal Abdul-Aziz. "I used to like Al Capone and the Lone Ranger because he had two guns. That was my character. The bigger the gun, the better. I wore double-breasted suits, suspenders, and a big Stetson hat. My gang made big money by robbing and stealing and extortion of store owners. I was a real gangster. The first time I shot somebody, I killed him."

A man sentenced to a life term can be kept in prison for the rest of his natural life, although in practice most lifers are eventually granted parole. Before 1979 a man sentenced to life in the state of New Jersey had to serve a minimum of 14.8 years in prison before he was considered eligible for parole. Since 1979 the law makes it mandatory for a lifer to serve a minimum of 30 years in prison. The courts can also stipulate that a lifer serve more than the minimum time. Some men serving life terms have stipulations of from 35 to 40 years, which means that they must serve at least that amount of time before they can be released. And since a lifer is seldom released the first time he is eligible for parole, most lifers usually expect to spend at least an additional 2 to 10 years beyond their minimum sentence before they have a reasonable chance for parole. Even when paroled, a lifer still remains under sentence and can be returned to prison if he violates the conditions of his parole. Only death frees him from his sentence.

While many people think of lifers as the most violent segment of the prison population, they are often among the most articulate, thoughtful, and well-educated in the prison

The kitchen and commissary provide the staples of prison life.

population. Lifers in general tend to take advantage of the programs offered in prison. Perhaps more than any other group, they educate themselves, turn to religion, seek counseling, learn jobs and skills, and try to turn their lives around. In part, this is due to the length of their sentence. The longer the time, the more they seek to fill it with meaningful activity. At the same time, the impact of a long sentence often has a profound impact on a man. Where the short-term criminal may consider prison to be an interlude in his life, and will pick up exactly where he left off before coming to prison, the lifer tends to reflect on his life and make some attempt to salvage what he can of it.

"Strange as it may sound," Abdul-Aziz reflects, "many of us who wound up in prison wanted to make a meaningful contribution. We wanted to go beyond the gravitational pull of our designated spots. But we didn't know how. Because of the inequality in our system, we were driven down certain roads. The pimp. The numbers runner. The robber. The drug dealer. They're the people who have always had the semblance of having it made. High unemployment. Our households run by women. No family structure. Confined to a certain geographical location in our community. My education, nil. What they were teaching me didn't apply to me. Into drugs. Into guns. We don't manufacture them, but they're in our community. Sometimes coming to jail can be a blessing."

Every lifer dreams of the day when he will leave prison and have another chance to do something with his life. "Getting out of here is the name of the game," lifer Imo Allen states. The lifer knows that if and when he gets out, it will probably be his last shot at a normal life. Should he fail, he will probably return to prison for the rest of his life. Whether or not he will be successful on the outside depends upon his motivation, the degree of insight he has gained into himself, the potential for violence within him, and the opportunities he finds for work and to build a stable family life.

The background of men serving life terms varies. Some lifers have grown up in jail, starting with juvenile detention homes and graduating to reformatories and eventually prison. A few lifers never committed a crime, except for the one that led to prison. Some were already career criminals at the age of seven. Others never got into trouble until they were thirty. Many come from poor, single-parent families and grew up wild in the streets. Some came from comfortable middle-class two-parent homes. While most men who commit crimes are white, most men in prison are black. In East Jersey State Prison, almost 80 percent of the population is black.

The fact that many men serving life terms at East Jersey State Prison become deeply involved in changing their lives has enabled them to become leaders within the prison. Today there are a number of organizations within the prison—the NAACP, the Prisoners Representative Committee, Penal Reform, the Islamic Affairs Council, the Rahway Forum Project, the Junior Chamber of Commerce, the Society for the Handicapped, and a Latin Representative Committee, among others. Many of these programs are run and staffed by men serving life sentences. This was not always the case, and it was out of the lack of meaningful programs that the Lifers' Group and the program that eventually came to be known as Scared Straight was born.

In 1976, in Trenton State Prison in New Jersey, a group

of men serving life sentences were concerned that there were not any significant programs for men serving life terms. Most of the programs were designed for prisoners serving short-term sentences. The lifers wanted to form a group that would be primarily for them. As Bob Conklin, one of the original lifers, remembers it: "The longer your sentence, the more your family falls off, the fewer people you know on the outside that can possibly lend you a helping hand. We said that we had to establish a lifeline between us and the community. We wanted to provide something for the family. The idea just kicked around and suddenly boomeranged into Scared Straight." Akbar Harris, who was incarcerated in Trenton at the time, remembers the thinking behind the program: "A few people had their own kids and that's what motivated them more. Some of their children were trying to emulate daddy. Guys said, 'damn, I can't have my kids doing what I do or come up behind me. Just 'cause I ran around with a gun or shot people, I can't have that happen to him. The world has more to offer him than a prison cell.' "

This idea became the germ for developing the Juvenile Awareness Program at East Jersey State Prison in which prisoners would use the tragedy of their own lives to help keep juveniles from following them. The Lifers' Group was formally set up and Sergeant Alan August, a young corrections officer and former golden gloves champion, and something of a maverick among prison officers, was assigned to be the liaison between the administration and the Lifers' Group. Schools and youth groups were invited to bring teenagers into the prison, where they could learn for themselves firsthand what it was like to serve time.

The Lifers' Group experimented with various approaches until finally they worked out a presentation that would ultimately gain them world fame. They brought teenage boys and girls who were getting into trouble onto a stage in the auditorium and in graphic, abusive language told them how they would be sexually, physically, and psychologically brutalized by the men and women inside if they came to prison. Then they made a point of counseling the youngsters, offering to help them with their problems or to get them help.

In 1979 a film was made about the program. Called *Scared Straight*, it focused on the abusive part of the program and minimized the counseling. The film brought praise from many parents, educators, psychologists, and even the young people themselves. It also brought some criticism. The objection was that young people cannot be "scared straight," that they need more than threats of violence to change their delinquent behavior. The Lifers' Group responded to the criticism by saying that they never said anyone would be changed just by being scared. They maintained that the heart of the program was, in fact, one-on-one counseling that often continued by mail or telephone over an extended period of time.

Today the program continues to flourish as some 2,500 young people are brought into the prison each year. Teenage girls no longer come to East Jersey State Prison but are taken to Clinton Prison, where the same program is run by women prisoners. In addition to the Juvenile Awareness Program, which is still aimed at youth in trouble, the Lifers' Group conducts a number of forums for high schools, colleges, and parent/adult groups. The forums are dialogues in which the audience is free to ask the lifers any questions they wish about

Work and play in the prison yard—some Lifers take time out for basketball.

their lives, prison, and the criminal justice system.

To be an active member of the Lifers' Group, a prisoner has to have a life sentence. Anyone with a sentence of twenty-five years or more can also join the group as an associate member. Associate members can head one of several committees of the lifers and several but not all of the executive offices. The total number of members averages between forty and fifty men.

To join the group, a man must file an application for membership, which is evaluated by a screening committee. The committee tries to eliminate anyone who has a pattern of getting into trouble in the prison or is a known dealer or heavy user of drugs. If the application is approved, the applicant is put on probation. During the probationary period, the new member observes the program and how each of the men makes his presentation. Some men specialize in describing the brutalities of prison life, while others emphasize educational and family values. At one time the probationary member would be asked to write an essay that was critiqued by the others in order to achieve simplicity and clarity of thought.

Once accepted by the group, a new member is assigned to one of the programs. Most members voluntarily make a small donation to the group of approximately $25 a year, which is used to pay the expenses of the program. No one is paid for his work with the Lifers' Group. For many men involvement can mean financial hardship, as they must devote a good deal of their time to the program, forfeiting part of a day's pay to do so. Being in the Lifers' Group does not lessen a man's sentence or contribute to his eligibility for parole.

Why do men join the Lifers' Group? Lifers' President

Harvey George sums up the feelings of many of the group. "For many of us, this group is our life inside prison. We live for this program! This is our chance to do something that we know is good, that we know is right, that we know will benefit some children, that we know will benefit us. You should understand that there are men in here, some of whom have committed terrible crimes, who want to do good, who want to do the right thing, but are afraid to or don't know how, or don't have the strength to. This doesn't excuse what they did, but that doesn't mean that what they did must deny them the chance to do something for themselves and for others. The program gives all of us a chance. It not only helps children change their lives for the better. It helps us, too."

"Where the hell do you think you are? This is a prison, not a schoolyard!"

THE HOUSE OF PAIN

CHAPTER 3

The school bus is late and Tim Reilly and his father are seated in the waiting room adjoining the entrance to the prison. Tim is fourteen years old, looks twelve, with a round, pudgy face and an earring in his right ear. He is wearing a sport shirt with the sleeves rolled up, khaki pants, Nike sneakers, and a baseball cap turned around so that the peak is backwards. He is smoking a cigarette and staring at the floor.

Seated opposite him is Eddie Reilly, his father. He has taken the day off without pay from his job as a driver for an express package service, and is angry with his son for having to do so. Desperate about his son's delinquent behavior, he has brought him to the Juvenile Awareness Program with the hope that perhaps "the convicts can shake his son up." The father is dressed as casually as his son. He is wearing a windbreaker, khaki pants, and a T-shirt. He is young enough to pass for the boy's older brother. From time to time, he glances at his son, who keeps his head bowed and will not meet his father's eyes.

Lieutenant Alan August enters the room from inside the prison and introduces himself. From his dress, he seems more like a successful businessman than a corrections officer. He is in his early forties, short and stocky, a chain-smoker, dressed in a designer suit with a sporty shirt open at the neck. His beard and mustache are trimmed and neat. He delights in the fact that some of his former boxing opponents are now in prison, both as officers and inmates.

Lieutenant August is the sole liaison between the prison and the Lifers' Group. While as a rule he does not interfere in the content, approach, or internal decisions of the prisoners, he closely oversees what goes on. He works more closely with the prisoners than any other officer in the prison. In the early days of the program, this created friction between him and some of his fellow officers who resented the publicity he was getting and the fact that he was friendly toward the prisoners. By involving some of the other officers in the program as well, he has since managed to reduce tension. Harvey George, president of the group, and several other lifers feel that "Augie is the cement that helps keep this program together."

Lieutenant August apologizes to the Reillys for the late start, explaining that he has to wait for a group of teenagers who will also be taken through the program. He asks Tim's father why he has brought his son.

"I don't know what to do with him anymore," his father complains. "He was arrested three weeks ago for malicious mischief and I have to go to court with him next week. He won't go to school, he drinks alcohol, smokes marijuana, comes home late and won't say where he's been. God knows what he's doing."

"I'm not doing nothing," Tim protests, without raising his head.

Lieutenant August suddenly turns to him and addresses him sharply. "What's the matter with you, are you stupid?"

Tim looks up.

"I'm asking you a question. Are you stupid?"

"No."

"You want to come to this place?"

"No."

" 'Cause once you get in a place like this, you can forget it. Nobody can help you. Not me. Not your papa. Nobody. There are only two things we do for you in this prison. Feed you and count you. Otherwise, you don't mean a thing to us. If somebody ices you—you know what ice means?"

Tim shakes his head.

"Ice—put you on ice—in the morgue. Understand?"

Tim nods his head without speaking.

"Speak to me, boy! What does it mean?"

"Kill you."

"That's right," the lieutenant continues. "Kill you. The other day, a man got killed over a cup. A stinking cup. And you know what it means to us? Another empty bed for the next guy to come in. Is that what you want?"

Tim shakes his head.

"Don't you listen to what your father tells you?"

"I don't know how to reach him anymore," Tim's father says. "We used to talk."

"What about his mother?" the lieutenant asks.

Both father and son are silent for a moment.

"His mother and I are divorced. She lives in Florida. She couldn't control him, so she sent him here to live with me."

"Is that what's bothering you, son?" The lieutenant's voice is suddenly kinder. Tim shrugs.

"Listen," he explains. "Those things happen. It's not

easy, but you got to put them behind you. And getting sent to prison isn't going to make things better."

"Is that still the problem?" his father asks. "The divorce?"

Tim bows his head and says nothing. Whatever he feels, he isn't telling. Anyone. Least of all his father.

Outside, a yellow school bus pulls up and twelve teenagers descend. They range in age from twelve to sixteen, although some seem as young as nine. They are less a group than a bunch of separate individuals thrown together. They are black, white, and Hispanic. Most of the black youths have

Lieutenant Alan August prepares teens who will be taken through the program.

slant or gummy haircuts, wear Gap pants, and Nike sneakers. The white youths have long hair, and are dressed in thin windbreakers and jackets. Several are wearing earrings. All have been brought to prison because they are getting into serious trouble. Some have been stealing cars or selling drugs, cutting school, and disrespecting their parents.

Lamont is the youngest. He is twelve but could pass for nine. He is four feet tall and weighs ninety-three pounds. He seems so frail and vulnerable that one wonders why he is here. Later on his counselor will tell the Lifers that he has been stealing cars since he was seven, that he terrorizes children younger than himself, and that for most of his life he has lived with a mother who is a drug addict and a prostitute. Now he is in a foster home.

Ernie is the oldest and is sixteen. Normally, he wears gold chains and walks with a swagger. He is a known gang leader. He has already been caught selling narcotics and guns and is considered to be extremely dangerous. He is the most hardened of the young people in the group. He pays no attention to what anyone says.

Tim joins the rear of the group, intimidated by and fearful of the others.

Henry is fourteen and has two bullet wounds in him from a policeman's gun. He has been part of a gang that steals cars and sells the parts. One car they stole happened to be used in a number of holdups and the police were looking for it. When they spotted it, they gave chase and the driver, thinking that the police were after them for stealing the car, tried to crash through a barricade that had been set up. The police opened fire and Henry was hit in the hand and thigh.

As they walk single file toward the waiting room, they are laughing and joking. Ernie is playing the fool and the tough guy. "I'm not gonna take nothing from nobody," he boasts. "Guy gets in my face, I'm gonna let him have it, con or no con." "Right on," someone calls out. The others laugh.

The teenagers are escorted into the corridor leading to the main doors to the prison. They are still playing around when Lieutenant August suddenly appears and shouts at them in a voice so loud and strong that its velocity makes them back up against the wall.

"Get up against the wall and shut up! Where the hell do you think you are! This is prison, not a school yard! Stand up straight, get your hands out of your pockets, and listen to me!"

Lieutenant August walks up and down the line, eyeing each of the youths. He comes to Ernie who, although intimidated, still has a sardonic look on his face. Lieutenant August reaches into the gym bag he's carrying and pulls out a cross. He hands it to Ernie.

"You. What's this?"

"A cross."

"Grab hold of it at the bottom here."

Ernie holds the bottom of the cross while Lieutenant August holds the top. "A guy in here had this on his wall, over his bed. Very religious fellow. Praying all the time. Never missed a church service."

The lieutenant stands back and separates the upper part of the cross from the lower. The upper part turns out to be the handle of a four-inch knife blade that is sheathed in the lower part of the cross. The teenagers are stunned.

Now you see it, now you don't—a four-inch knife blade is hidden in a wooden cross.

"Nice, huh?" the lieutenant asks.

Again he reaches into his bag and pulls out weapon after weapon. Knives made out of paint rollers, screwdrivers, nail files, nails, pieces of scrap metal, and sharpened pieces of wood. He holds up a zip gun.

"These are the weapons that we find in here, that guys make in here. Rather, these are the weapons that the prisoners let us find. These don't worry us. What worries us are the weapons that we don't find. There are twenty-two hundred guys in here. There may be twenty-two hundred weapons we don't know about. Sometimes we find a weapon during a routine check. Most of the time we find a weapon because it's sticking in some guy."

The teenagers are silent now. Lieutenant August has got their attention. He leads them through the first set of doors they are to pass through before entering the main prison area. First they will be inspected to make sure they are not carrying contraband items into the prison, items such as money, jewelry, weapons, or drugs. The room is sealed at both ends by heavy metal doors that can only be opened or closed by an officer in the control room that adjoins the inspection room. Only one door at a time can be opened. In this way, if someone tries to escape, he can be cut off by the second door.

The door slams shut behind them and the teenagers are frisked by an officer, as is everyone who enters this room, including the superintendent. They then pass through the second door and into a space that is separated from the main prison by a wire fence and another gate. As they enter, they see hundreds of men moving from one area to another. They must wait until the movement is over before they pass in, because there is always a risk that someone may try to break out through an open door when there is a mass movement.

As they wait, the teenagers are lined up against the wire fence. It is a harrowing moment. They are insulted and taunted by some of the men who pass by on the other side of the fence. Much of the abuse is deliberate. Many who are not in the lifers' program support its aims, so that their remarks are intended to shake up the youngsters rather than to threaten them. But it is hard to know who is acting and who is sincere. Tim is visibly shaken, as are most of the other youths.

When the movement is over, the teenagers enter into the prison where six lifers are waiting for them. There are no handshakes, no friendly greetings. The faces of the lifers are grim, their voices loud. They are met by Ned Woodley, a short, powerfully built man, so muscular that he seems as wide as he is tall. He can bench press 450 pounds. When he speaks, they listen. He is like a marine drill sergeant, barking out commands. He notices Ernie's sarcastic smile and walks over to him and puts his face so close to Ernie's that the teenager leans back.

"What are you smiling about, boy?"

"Nothing."

"If you think's something's funny, let's hear you laugh."

"I'm not laughing."

"If you got a beef, let's hear it."

"I got no beef."

"Maybe you think that because you're on tour, nothing's gonna happen to you. Maybe you're right. But maybe you're wrong. You never know in here what a guy will do. Or maybe the day will come when I'll see you in here and wipe that smile off your face. 'Cause there ain't nothing funny in here. You know what this place is? The House of Pain. This is the House of Pain! You got me?"

"Yes, sir."

"Don't 'sir' me, punk. I ain't no police officer. Now get back in line."

The lifers escort the youths into Four Wing, where they are watched by men whose expressions reveal nothing of what they are thinking and feeling. They line the youths up in front of the cells. Some of them are occupied and the men inside coldly regard the youths. Some of the cells are empty and closed.

"I want you to look inside," Pete Foster says. "Eyes straight ahead. For some of us, this is our home for the next twenty-five years. It can be yours, too."

Pete signals and the cell doors open on the closed cells. Several of the men who are in cells step out.

"Get in there," Dawud Abdul-Wasi orders Tim. "Get in there before somebody knocks you in there."

A small, middle aged, mild-looking man, who looks like somebody's kind uncle, politely invites Tim to inspect his cell. "You see. I did terrible things when I was a young man. I killed three men. Now I must spend the rest of my life here." Tim is visibly shaken by what he says. It is hard for him to associate such violence with such a frail-looking man.

Ned Woodley calls out and the cell doors are locked. Tim feels a momentary sense of panic. He wants to cry and call out to his father to make them open the door. Instead, he looks around. He sees pictures of the man's family on the wall, a cross that reminds him of the cross containing a knife, and next to the cross, pictures of the Pope. Clothes are neatly hung up. After a minute passes by, the cell doors are opened.

The teenagers are then taken to solitary confinement, where Pete Foster explains what it's like to spend almost every hour of every day by yourself behind bars—the loneliness, the boredom, the monotony. Then the group is taken to the shower room where a man was recently knifed to death. Dawud Abdul-Wasi grabs Tim and demonstrates with his closed fist where the knife blade went into the dead man's body—in his back and neck.

"You know what it was over?" he asks. "A drinking cup. One guy picked up the other guy's drinking cup when he left it behind and wouldn't return it. So the other guy waited till he was taking a shower, and when the water was all hot and steamy he stuck him. Ruptured his heart. That's the value system we have in here."

The teenagers are marched quick-step out of the wing and into an auditorium where twelve other lifers are waiting for them. The youths are hurried up the steps and onto a stage, lined up, and addressed. Then, suddenly, from the rear of the stage, a voice booms out and a man steps forward, out of the darkness.

"This is our home for the next twenty-five years. It can be yours, too."

THE STAGE

CHAPTER 4

"**M**y name is 62098 and my sentence is double life! That means I'm going to die in this stinking prison. I've been in prison thirty-two out of my fifty-three years. When I was born, my mother gave me the name of Christopher because it reminded her of Jesus Christ. In prison, they call me 'Crazy Chris.' "

In a darkened auditorium, with only a few dim lights on the stage, "Crazy Chris," looms over the twelve teenagers. A giant of a man, 6-feet 3-inches tall, 240 pounds, with arms as thick as most men's legs, he is tattooed from shoulder to wrist. Fourteen other intense, angry-looking men, all serving life sentences, are seated on the stage opposite the youths whose swaggers and smiles are gone. The teenagers stare at the floor.

In an anguished and loud voice, Chris begins his presentation. "This program is called Juvenile Awareness," his voice booms through the auditorium. "Its purpose is to make you aware of the stupid stuff you're doing and what can happen to you if you don't get your act together." Chris suddenly interrupts himself. "Let's get one thing straight, you little mothers! When I'm talking, **all eyes on me**! I don't want you looking at your shoes. I don't want you looking up to heaven. No angel's coming down to rescue you anyhow. I want to see your eyes or I'll knock you off this stage. Is that clear?"

The teenagers are too terrified to reply.

"I said is that clear! Let me hear your answer!"

"Yes." Twelve voices speak as one.

"This is prison. This is my house! *I gotta live here. I've been incarcerated in my cell for thirty-two of my fifty-three years!* They made me lose my mind. Because I didn't listen. Because I wouldn't listen. And if you don't listen, then you're gonna come to this place. I'm your friend now because I'm trying to teach you something, to keep you out of prison. But if you don't listen today, then I'll be waiting here for you. And I'll no longer be your friend. I'll be your worst nightmare come to life, except I ain't no dream you can wake up from. And when a guy like me comes into your cell, I'm gonna use you. I'm gonna abuse you. You like to wash clothes? Good, because you're going to wash my socks and underwear. You drink coffee? So do I. You'll go to the dining room every morning at six thirty and bring me mine. You get cookies from home? Good, I like cookies. You smoke Marlboros? Change your brand because I smoke Winstons. How do you think your mama's gonna feel when you ask her for a size twelve pair of shoes and she knows you wear size nine? If you don't do it, I'm gonna stick you. And if I don't, somebody else will. It'll happen maybe on the day the guard will yell 'shower.' How are you going to feel with fifty guys watching you as you walk into the shower with a towel around you, waiting for you to remove it. Guys have been in here five to twenty years and here you come, a little tenderoni, the closest thing they've seen to a woman since they've been here—fifty sick guys. And someone will turn the shower up so its nice and hot and there's a lot of steam. Then suddenly, a fist cuts through the steam and crashes into your face and you're knocked out. And you know what happens to you then.

"And there's nobody to help you. Not mama, not papa, not the guards, not the superintendent, or the governor. Not only do you have to suffer inside, but you begin to lose contact with the world outside. One day your papa, he don't want to have anything to do with you. Your brothers and sisters are ashamed of you. Your friends. You find out you ain't got any friends. Mama remains loyal maybe, but she ain't gonna live forever and what you've done is killing her anyhow. Your girls, your wives, they cut out on you. It's hard to wait. One day I called my wife after I had been here six years. Some guy answered the phone. I hang up thinking maybe I got the wrong number, that I dialed one digit wrong. So I called again, making sure I dialed the right number. This time she answers the phone. I don't say, 'Hi, how are you? How's the kid? Gee, honey, I miss you.' No, I start accusing her right away of shacking up with some guy while I'm in prison. She says, 'Hey, I didn't ask you to go to prison. I didn't ask you to sell dope. I didn't ask you to be a dope fiend. I didn't ask you to kill anybody. What I asked you was to get a job and support me and the baby. So I met someone who's willing to do that. He reminded me of you before you did all those things. So do me a favor. Don't call me anymore. Don't write me. I don't want you to contact me or the kid. Just think of us as dead.' "

Perspiration flows down Chris's face as he finishes his story. His tattooed arms are soaking wet. For the first time he begins to speak in a soft voice. For the first time the boys on stage begin to lose some of their fear of him. "When she said that, it tore through me. I wanted to rip the phone off the wall and beat someone over the head with it. It hurt real bad. It's the worst pain in the world." He stops for a moment. It is hard to tell if his eyes are covered with sweat or tears. "And that's when you find out that you're not as tough as you thought you

Chris demands that teens look in his eyes when he tells them: "I'm gonna die in this place!"

were. And you look in the mirror and say, who the hell is that guy with all that gray in his beard and those wrinkles in his face?" Suddenly, Chris cries out, *"I'm losing it! I'm losing my mind!* And there's no salvation, because they don't want to let me out no more. I'm gonna die in this place."

Chris walks off the stage and his place is taken by Willie Allen, known as "Big Al" to his friends. Tall, extremely articulate, thirty-six years old, Willie Allen has spent eighteen of his last twenty years in jail. Like Chris, drugs were his downfall. He begins his presentation by passing out the lifers' identification cards to the youngsters as he speaks:

"These are our identification cards. This is to show you who we are. Prisoners. We ain't no social workers. We ain't no counselors. We ain't no police. We're cons ... lifers ... and we've spent most of our lives in prison." Willie turns to the men seated behind him and like a drill sergeant he goes down the row rapidly asking each the same question.

"How much time you got?"

"Life!"

"How much time you got?"

"Natural life!"

"Time you got?"

"Life plus thirty years!"

"Time?"

"Twenty-five years!"

"How much time?"

"Forty years!"

Willie now turns to the line and selects one of the teenagers and makes him stand up in front of the others.

"What's your name?"

"Ernie."

"What you here for?"

"Selling."

"Selling what? Don't play the fool with me, boy."

"Drugs."

"What drugs you selling?"

"Cocaine."

"Who you selling it to? Your own people?"

"Yes."

Willie looks down the line and pulls out another teenager who stands next to Ernie.

"What's your name?"

"Clarence."

Willie turns to Ernie. "Suppose Ernie here sells a bag of dope to your little sister? What are you going to do?"

"Kill him," Clarence answers dryly.

Willie looks at Clarence to see if he is bluffing. He is not.

"You're gonna kill him, huh? What for? You're selling his little sister dope. Why shouldn't he sell it to yours? Or is it okay for him to kill you for what you're doing?" Clarence does not answer.

"How old are you, Clarence?"

"Fourteen."

"Come over here. I want you to meet somebody." He takes him over to a young black man seated on the bench.

"How much time you doing, Calvin?"

"Life with a thirty-year stip."

"You know what that means?"

Clarence shakes his head.

Willie Allen explains. "That means he's got to spend

thirty years here before he can even be considered for parole." He turns back to Calvin.

"How old when you were sentenced?"

"Fourteen."

Willie turns to Clarence. "How old did you say you are, Clarence?"

"Fourteen."

"Are you ready to serve thirty years?"

"No."

"Then why would you kill him?"

" 'Cause he disrespected my sister."

"Even though you dissed his?"

Clarence says nothing.

"I look at your faces and my heart aches. I look at your anger and it tears me up inside. You're angry with us because we're trying to do something for you. You're angry with your mamas and papas because they're trying to help you. You're angry with your teachers, because they're trying to get something into your heads. You know where all the bad things are, but you don't know where success is. You know how much reefer costs, but you can't add or subtract. You know where you can get a bag of dope or crack, but you don't know where the library is. You know what a nine mil pistol is, but you can't read like you should. It's a shame you can't walk down the street going to school without somebody thinking you're going to rob them. Don't you know what's going down? There's a war on the streets and it's against you. It's against all juveniles. They don't like you. They don't like you 'cause you sell crack, or you use it, and carry guns and knives and kill people. They don't like the way you dress, the way you walk

Tariq Commander ominously describes the-man-in-the-next-cell.

and the way you talk and the way you wear your hair. When are you going to wake up to what's happening?"

Willie Allen steps down and Tariq Commander rises and takes over. He is a large, angry-looking man who speaks with the eloquence, power, and rhythm of a preacher. He walks over to Tim and stares at him for a moment. Tim smiles nervously at him.

"What's your name?"

"Tim."

"Tim, you like to smile. What are you smiling about?"

"Nothing."

"Nothing, huh. Let me tell you something, Tim. If you come into this hellhole, and be in the cell next to someone who's serving ninety-nine years, who has a serious attitude problem and doesn't care whether he lives or dies, 'cause he knows he's only leaving this place with a tag on his toes—you get the drift—and he sees you smile, he'll want to know what you're smiling about. And he's going to ask you that as he puts his shank in your head. He's gonna ask you, 'What's funny now, Tim?' That's the way the game is played in here."

The intensity of Tariq's description makes it painful for Tim to look at him directly. He bows his head only to have Tariq suddenly snap at him.

"Look at me, boy!"

Tim forces himself to meet Tariq's penetrating gaze.

"What are you learning in school, Tim?"

"Nothing."

"Why not?"

"The teachers are no good."

"But there's nothing wrong with you, right? You're

good. It's the teachers that are bad. Is that what you're saying?"

"Yes," Tim replies weakly.

"You can't learn in school, so you have to come to a maximum security prison to learn. What's the matter with you, boy? What do you think you can learn here?"

"To stay out of prison," he says weakly. He is close to tears and Tariq senses it. He bears down on Tim.

"Who do you love, Tim?"

Tim shrugs.

"Does that mean no one?"

He shrugs again.

"So then it's all right if I knock your head off."

"No," Tim protests.

"Why not? You just told me you don't love nobody. That means you don't love yourself. That's what the problem is. You don't love yourself. You don't respect yourself. So you can't respect your parents, who care about you. You can't respect your teacher, who wants to give you something up here in your head. You can't respect your friends, because you don't give a damn about yourself. That's what the problem is." Tariq leads Tim up to the bench so that he is almost touching the men seated there. "You see what you got here, Tim? Men who didn't respect themselves, and who didn't respect anybody else. You're looking at a bunch of losers. You're looking at a bunch of guys who sold their lives out, doing the dumb stuff you're doing. We thought we could make an easy living. Just go in and stick up a store. We didn't need an education. We thought we didn't need nobody to guide us, to give us some direction in our life. We had it. We sold out. We sold out on ourselves. We sold out on the people who loved us, because they had something better in mind for us than prison. We sold out on our wives and kids, because we weren't there to be husbands and fathers to them. We sold out on everything—except for doing time. All we can teach you up here is how to lose. We can tell how to lose. We can't tell you how to make it because we ain't successful at making it. Your teacher tries to teach you how to operate a computer—to put some data in and take some data out. In here all I can teach you is how to put some steel in a man and take some steel out. That's my world. *That's my world*!

"You look like a good little kid. You're all not bad kids. But you make bad choices. You want to make your mark on the world. You want to be understood. You want to relate to somebody, somewhere, somehow, but you just don't know how to do it. You think bomber jackets and gold chains and Air Jordan sneakers is gonna make you popular. You dress up your hair, the head is dressed up—but there's nothing in the mind. The mind is not dressed up. You live in a ghetto, but the ghetto is in your head. You got to take the graffiti of prejudice out of your mind. You got to take the graffiti of degradation and oppression out of your mind and work toward your potential. You still have a chance to be anything you want to be. Doctors, lawyers, judges. But if you want to be a convict, you can be that, too. We're trying to wake you up to the reality that you could do more with your life than what you are doing."

Bilal Abdul-Aziz takes Tariq's place. His manner is mild, almost gentle. A deeply committed member of the Nation of Islam, Bilal Abdul-Aziz considers himself "blessed" that he came to prison. "If I had stayed on the streets the way I was, I would have been killed."

Before he speaks, Abdul-Aziz looks at the young faces in front of him. They are subdued and quiet. He is struck by how young they look. His voice is mellow, almost pleading.

"We're not up here to pick on you. We're up here to prevent you from becoming a statistic, as we are. Look at these guys. Look at their faces real good. What you're looking at when you see these guys' faces is pain and suffering. They average nineteen years in jail. Nineteen years! There's no way to ever get that back. Do you understand that? Do you know you

By now, the Lifers, including Ned Woodley . . .

are being blessed today? That somebody might say something that may save your lives? You might hear something you might never again hear in your life."

Abdul-Aziz walks over to Lamont, the youngest and the frailest of the group and pulls him out of line.

"What you here for today? What did you do?"

"Steal a car."

"Steal a car? How do you drive a car? When you get in the car, what do you do? How do your feet reach the pedals? You're so small, how can you look through the steering wheel? You stand up on the seat?"

have an attentive audience.

"I sit."

"How do you see?"

"I put the floor mats on the seat."

"And how do you operate the pedals? Your feet can't reach them."

"My friend does."

"So you steer the car and your honcho works the brakes and gas pedal. Is that it?"

"Yes."

"And what do you do with the car?"

"We drive around the school yard."

"How old are you?"

"Twelve."

"And how old were you when you started stealing cars?"

"Seven."

"So you been a car thief since you were seven. Is that right?"

"Yes."

"Your peers, your homeboys, they respect you when you steal cars?"

"Yeah."

"They look up to you. Why are you in the frame of mind that in order to be recognized, you got to do something stupid? Because nobody will recognize you when you do stuff right?"

Lamont is silent.

"Talk to me!" Lamont is startled at the sudden burst of power in Abdul-Aziz's voice.

"Yes."

Abdul-Aziz notices the boy standing next to him looking at Lamont. He pulls him out of line and stands him next to Lamont.

"What's your name?"

"Henry."

"How old are you?"

"Thirteen."

"Why you here?"

"I got shot by the police."

Abdul-Aziz is stunned. "How did you get shot by the police?"

"I was in a car that was stolen and the police was chasing it and I got shot."

"Where did they shoot you?"

"In the ankle and thigh."

"You didn't know the car was stolen?"

"No."

"Don't lie to me, boy. Did you ask when you got into the car whose car was it?"

"No."

"You just got in with your friends and you didn't even bother to find out where they got the car. You couldn't be that stupid."

"Yes."

"You're a sucker, you know that! You're nothing but a damn fool and if you don't believe me, look at your ankle and your thigh. But you learned your lesson of course. Am I right? If one of your honchos drove up today and they was in a car, you'd ask them where they got the car before you got in. Am I right?"

"Yes."

"You're a damn liar!" Abdul-Aziz's voice suddenly becomes soft and gentle, filled with compassion and understanding. He speaks low and yet every word can be heard clearly throughout the silent auditorium. His eyes are on Lamont and Henry, but he is speaking to all the boys on the stage.

"Don't you know somebody's setting a trap for you? If you're up on it, you can avoid the trap. Is it just a coincidence that everybody you know is into something foul? Stealing cars. Selling dope. Guns. B&E [breaking and entering]. Uzis. And that somewhere down the line a bullet is waiting for you with your name on it. That someone is determined to wipe you out before you reach my age. But you do know that, don't you? You playing the game right along with them. Because somewhere in the back of your mind you feel that life isn't worth living. You don't see a place for yourselves in this world. Because you believe you belong in prison anyway."

Lamont is trembling. Henry is silent and without being aware of it is rubbing the spot on his ankle where the bullet hit him. It is totally quiet in the auditorium.

"Don't you know what you're doing to folks that love you?"

Lamont mumbles a few words that cannot be heard. One of the lifers calls for him to speak out.

"I live in a foster home," he says.

Bending down so that he is facing this frail, trembling child on the stage, Abdul-Aziz gently asks, "Nobody love you there? Is that what you're saying?"

Lamont nods. He is close to tears and afraid that he will cry if he speaks.

"How 'bout you? Do you love yourself?"

Lamont shakes his head.

"Well, at least you're honest. How's anybody going to love you if you don't love yourself?"

Lamont shakes his head again.

"What about the people that brought you here to this program today? Don't they love you?"

Lamont shrugs.

"Answer me. Don't they love you?"

"I don't know."

"Why do you think they brought you here, if they didn't love you?" Abdul-Aziz stands up and faces the others. "All of you, why do you think that your counselors brought you here today, if they didn't love you?" He pauses. "And why do you think we talk to you today?"

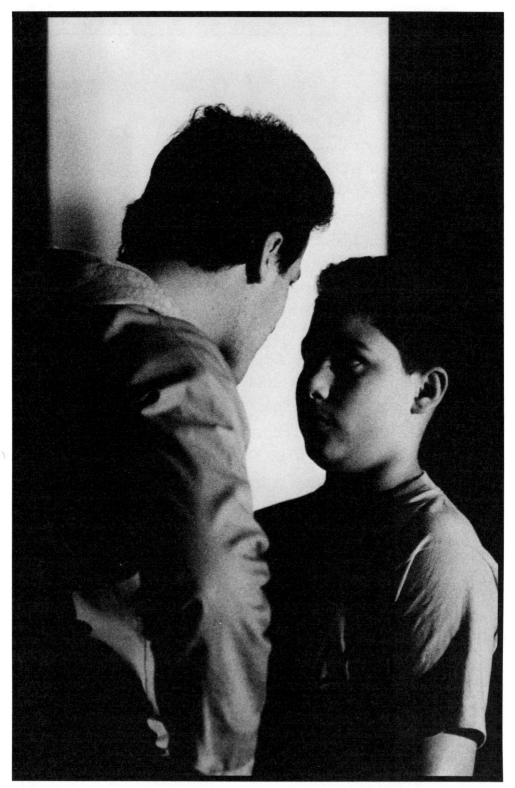

"One-on-One" means getting a teen to build a bridge between himself and someone who will help him.

ONE-ON-ONE

CHAPTER 5

The main presentation has ended and each lifer now takes one of the youngsters aside and talks with him alone. For the lifers, this is the most important part of the day's presentation. It is their chance to make contact with the teenagers and although the lifers know how difficult it is going to be for them to change. Most have grown up without a father. Some have been physically and emotionally abused. Almost all of them live in areas where the drug dealer and the hit man are role models and drug addicts are part of the landscape. The hope of the Lifers' Group is to build a bridge between themselves and the young people or at least encourage them to build a bridge with those who can help them.

Dawud Abdul-Wasi is talking with Jeff, who has been using and selling drugs for almost two years. Abdul-Wasi is a tall, thin man, the imam (religious leader) of the Sunni Muslim community at Rahway and a former member of both the

Prisoners Representative Committee and the Latino Representative Committee. A man who "once loved to smoke reefer," his deep commitment to Islam led him to put aside drugs and what he calls "the hypocritical life" and strive to become a righteous man.

"You dealing in the streets?" he asks Jeff.

"A little."

"So you're playing the game?"

Jeff shrugs.

"If you're playing the game, there are things you need to know, aren't there?"

"What do you mean?"

"Do you know the rules of the game you're playing? How much time do you get for selling drugs if you get caught?"

Jeff shakes his head.

"Two years, mandatory minimum. Do you know what mandatory minimum means?"

"No."

"It means you got to serve that much time before you are eligible for parole. How much time do you get if you are caught selling drugs within a thousand feet of a school?"

"I don't know."

"Three to five years. Here you are playing the game and you don't even know the rules? The ultimate rule is death. Didn't you hear Calvin say that he got a life sentence with a thirty-year stipulation when he was only fourteen years old? How old's your mom?"

"Thirty-two."

"She'll be over sixty years old when Calvin is eligible—

mind you, eligible—for release. And he may not make it even then."

In another section of the auditorium, John Chaney talks with Darryl, a sullen thirteen-year-old boy who sat silently on the stage and said nothing. Chaney is aware that Darryl has a great deal of difficulty with his parents. At first Darryl is extremely reluctant to talk about his family. But under Chaney's gentle questioning, Darryl confesses that he is beaten by his stepfather.

"Why should he be beating you if you're doing the right thing?"

"He just does."

Chaney suspects there is more to this story than Darryl is telling.

"Has he been abusing you?"

Darryl shrugs.

"You know what abusing means?"

"Yeah."

"Has he been molesting you?"

The boy says nothing.

"Have you told anybody else about this?"

Darryl shakes his head.

"Well, how in the world do you expect to solve the problem, unless you tell somebody about it? Don't you know someone outside you can have that kind of a conversation with? If you realize you need help, you have to seek help. Help doesn't seek you. You have to find it."

John Chaney does not probe into the details of Darryl's problem. Instead he encourages him to find someone he can trust to help him find a way to deal with it. Darryl says he has an aunt he can trust and that he will talk it over with her. He promises to write John and tell him what happens. John suspects that Darryl will not write but that maybe he will talk things over with his aunt. He warns Darryl that if he does not solve his problem, the anger within him will one day explode and he may seriously hurt or kill someone—and wind up in prison. "And that's no solution to your problem," he adds.

Joey Mackiewicz has taken Tim Reilly aside, while his father, who sits on the opposite side of the auditorium, watches him anxiously. Joey, suspecting that Tim is drinking more than he will admit to, tells him about his own unhappy

Tariq tells it . . .

life as an alcoholic. While most men are reluctant to talk about their crimes to strangers, some, like Joey, do so when they feel it may help a young person. For Joey, his willingness to speak to young people about his own life is a personal triumph, for he is basically a shy man whose tendency is to keep things to himself. Being in the Lifers' Group has helped him articulate his own thoughts and feelings to others and encouraged him to change his own life.

Joey confesses to Tim that his alcoholism led him to kill a man in a fight and that his problem with alcohol was intensified by peer pressure. When he was the same age as Tim, all

like it is.

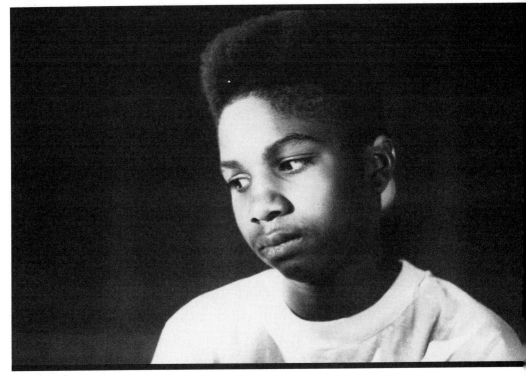

his friends were drinking heavily and to be part of the group he began to drink. By the time Joey was sixteen, he was an alcoholic.

"What type of guys do you hang around with?" Joey asks Tim.

"Punkers. Skinheads."

"Why skinheads?"

"I like the music." Joey senses that there is another element.

"Because they don't like blacks?"

Tim is silent.

"Don't think I'm gonna be sympathetic to that. I don't like skinheads. They come in here and pull their crap, they'll get it from me before any black guys get to them. You see us here in the Lifers' Group, black, white, Latino—all races and religions. What do you think will happen to you if you come in prison with an attitude toward black people?"

"I'll get hurt," Tim says.

"That's right. So what do you have to do then?"

"Stay out of prison."

"How you gonna stay out of prison with the life you're leading? I know what you're doing. Everything you're doing, I did. School was for the birds. Right? So I cut school. Hang out with the cool crowd? I was a gang member. Drink? I was an alcoholic. Then one day I needed money for a drink. I was in a guy's apartment who I didn't know very well and I tried to steal money from him when I thought he wasn't looking. He caught me and I beat him up. I didn't mean to kill him or really hurt him. I was just protecting myself. Well, he died from the beating. You think that could happen to you?"

As Joey tells his story, Tim is deeply attentive.

"I don't think so," Tim replies.

"I didn't think so, either," Joey says flatly. "And look where I am today."

As Joey talks with Tim, José Perez is standing talking to Vincent about school. A slow, inarticulate boy, Vincent has trouble looking Jose in the eye.

"Why don't you like school?"

" 'Cause I don't get good grades."

"Why don't you get good grades?"

"I don't know. 'Cause I'm stupid."

Perez suddenly explodes, startling Vincent.

"Don't you ever say that about yourself, man! You hear me? I don't ever want to hear you down on yourself. That's the trouble with black and Latino people. They give up on themselves. You got to make an effort, man. You got to start believing in yourself."

Nearby, Tariq Commander is talking with Henry, the youth who was shot by the police. Henry tells Tariq that he seldom stays at home because he does not get along with his mother. He complains that she's always on his case, demanding that he do things he doesn't want to do.

"Like take out the garbage?" Tariq asks.

"Yeah."

"What do you do when she asks?"

"I take it out."

"Why?"

" 'Cause she asks."

"What do you say?"

"Nothing."

"Yes you do. You say 'kiss my butt.' Your lips may not say it, but that's what's going on in your head."

Henry bows his head.

"Why do you think she asks you to take out the garbage?"

" 'Cause she don't want to do it."

"You let the lesson go by. You let it slip away from you. The lesson is to teach you responsibility, that you have a job in the family, more than just sliding your feet under the table and sticking your hand in the refrigerator. Your mom is praying that someday the responsibility of taking out the garbage will transfer to your being just as responsible in society. Your problem is that you want to be a man before your time. That was the problem of all of us in here. We wanted to be men before we was ready to be men. We thought we was slick. We thought we was cool. Just like you. And here we are. And here you'll be, if you keep up doing the same stupid stuff that you've been doing. What do you learn in life if not from your mother. You learn your culture at the knees of your mother."

In a corner of the auditorium, Pete Foster and Willie Allen have their hands full with Ernie, who has an attitude that they are trying to break through.

"What's the matter with you?" Willie asks. "You think we were kidding on stage?"

"This program is all right for these other guys." Ernie replies. "It's just not for me."

"Why not?" Pete Foster asks.

"I'm beyond that, man. I'm already on my way. I already got my own gang. They obey me when I tell them what to do."

"What makes you and your gang so special?" Pete asks.

" 'Cause you got to shoot a man to be a member. And if you kill a man, you become a captain, like me."

"What!" Willie is stunned. "Do you know what you're saying?"

"Look, I hear you and I understand what you're saying and what you're trying to do. But on the streets today, you ain't nothing till you killed a man. That's the way it is."

Later on Willie sadly concludes, "We just got to accept that we can't save them all. If we save just one, we're lucky. If Ernie's gonna learn anything, it's gonna be in here."

After the program, the youths return to the van and begin to joke around. On the ride back, the counselor who brought them asks what impression Scared Straight made on them. The younger children say it affected them and they don't want to go to prison. Several say they will write to the men they met, but there is no real sincerity in their voices. Others say it will make them think about things. Ernie says nothing. He is already thinking about the street and what he will do there when he returns later on that evening.

As Tim rides home with his father, they sit silently side by side. The program has deeply affected him. He has been scared by the thought of going to prison and encouraged by his conversation with Joey. He has decided that he will write him and make an effort to get his life together. But he will not tell his father this. At least, not now.

His mom was ready to put him away, but she called the Lifers' Group first.

TURNED AROUND

CHAPTER 6

Does the program work? If it does not save everyone who comes through, it has changed the lives of many. And sometimes it can have an effect on those whose lives almost seem beyond redemption.

"The program saved my life," Abdul-Kareem states without hesitation. "No question about it. I first saw the program when I was fourteen. It scared me, but I forgot about it soon after. Drugs was my life. I lived for getting high. I was high all the time. Cocaine. I was using a lot of the stuff. I didn't care about school. I didn't care about nothing but drugs."

In 1988 Kareem was riding on a train with several friends. He had managed to secure some cocaine and was not aware that the police were looking for the friends he was with. When they were picked up by the police, Kareem was arrested along with the others. "I was so high that I refused to get rid of the drugs I had. I believed that somehow the police would not search me." They did and Kareem was sentenced to time in the county jail.

"For the first time, I began to think about myself. What if I had gotten years instead of months? Or a long sentence? I could never do the time. No way. And yet drugs was still a big temptation for me."

As part of his sentence, Kareem was ordered to attend the Juvenile Awareness Program again. This time he met Dawud Abdul-Wasi and they exchanged greetings in Arabic. "I was studying Islam and had become a Muslim. I felt an instant kinship for Abdul-Wasi. When I got back to the halfway house I was staying in, I sent him a letter asking if I could write to him. We began to exchange letters. He became my role model and teacher. I can talk to him about anything. When I don't understand the religion, he explains it to me. If I got a problem about something, we talk it over. Every Wednesday we talk on the phone, but I call him whenever I feel like talking to him."

Since he has been in the program, Kareem's life has changed dramatically. He returned to school and was elected to the school leadership council. He has been invited to lecture throughout New Jersey to other students in other schools about his life. Recently, he graduated from high school and has been accepted to college.

Elizabeth Villano was on the verge of having her son Jimmy committed until she tried the Lifers' Group. "I was ready to put him away. Anywhere. I just couldn't handle him. You couldn't talk to him. He was out drinking, hanging around with bad kids, staying out late at night and not letting me know where he was. He was playing hooky and failing in school. He was headed for prison." Jimmy agrees with his mother. "I was angry with my father for having left me when I was small and did not get along with my stepfather. So I just wanted to get out of the house and hang out. I didn't care about anything."

Through a friend, Elizabeth Villano contacted the Juvenile Awareness Program. The man she talked to was Hakeem Shakoor, an executive officer of the group. He arranged for her to bring Jimmy to the program. Once was enough. "I was scared, but I also liked and respected the guys," Jimmy recalls. "I could relate to them and what they were saying."

Hakeem began to keep in touch with Jimmy by phone. Although he still wouldn't communicate with his mother, Jimmy would talk with Hakeem. If he wanted to go to a party and his mother was wary about letting him do so, Hakeem and Jimmy would talk it over. Then Hakeem would talk with Jimmy's mother and work out a compromise, while encouraging Jimmy to try and talk with his mother. Jimmy began to change. He stopped playing hooky, improved his grades, stopped drinking, and cut back on hanging out. "He's got a way to go, but I see a big improvement," Elizabeth Villano has observed. "The lifers really helped my son."

Hakeem tells of a phone conversation he recently had with Kay Rodgers, a thirty-five-year-old single parent, about her sixteen-year-old son Kyle. Her son's parole officer had suggested that she write. Hakeem then spoke with her over the telephone. At first she was calm, but as she told her story, her voice trembled and Hakeem sensed she was close to tears.

Kay Rodgers told him that her son had become wild and she could no longer control him. "He's out on the streets. He hangs out with some kids that steal cars. He doesn't come home some nights. He won't talk to me or tell me what he's doing. He goes to Philadelphia without permission. He steals money from me to play video games at the local arcade. Two months ago he was shot, but he won't tell me what it's about. He says it was an accident. He's cutting school. He won't listen to me. He says he can make his own decisions. Now he wants to leave here and go to Philadelphia and live with his friends."

Kay Rodgers told Hakeem that she had a good job as a secretary, was studying at night at a local college, and at the same time trying to raise a teenage son on her own. "Rich, poor, white, black," Hakeem noted, "it doesn't make any difference. Ninety-nine out of a hundred times, the mother's going to have trouble when there's no father around."

Elizabeth Villano was certain that her son was headed for prison . . .

Hakeem suggested to Kay Rodgers that she ask Kyle to call him and let them speak in private. Normally he would suggest that she bring him to the program, but since she lived a long distance away, she was not sure that Kyle would make the trip. That evening she called Hakeem and put her son on the phone, without telling him who he was talking to. Hakeem introduced himself right away. "My name is Hakeem Shakoor. I am serving a life term in East Jersey State Prison on a charge of homicide." He briefly explained the Lifers' Group

Hakeem Shakoor wasn't so sure. He began to keep in touch.

and then continued. "Your mother called me because she said you and her were having trouble and she thought that maybe you might be willing to talk about some of the problems you've been having."

Surprisingly, Kyle opened up almost immediately. There was something fascinating to him about talking to a man in prison, especially someone serving a life term. He imagined Hakeem to be someone he could boast about to his friends. For ten minutes they talked. Kyle told Hakeem that he hated where he was living, a small city without much to do—except get into trouble. He was not getting along with the kids in school and his teachers. The only excitement was hanging out in the streets with older guys. If he had a choice, he'd rather be back in Philadelphia with his friends. Hakeem was sympathetic. Realizing there was little he could do until he established a rapport with Kyle, he asked if he would make a trip to the prison with his mother to go through the program and then meet afterwards. Kyle agreed. Visiting a maximum security prison, he thought, would help him get a "rep" with his friends.

Two weeks later Kyle and his mother visited the prison and Kyle was taken through the program. After the program, Hakeem and Kyle talked together.

"Tell me, you think you can do time here? The truth."

Kyle shakes his head.

"Well, if you can't do time here, why are you doing your best to get yourself in this place? 'Cause that's where you're headed. You know the pain you cause your mother, don't you. She suffered pain to bring you into the world and here you are, almost grown, and you continue to cause her pain. Why is it that so many young men always tell our mothers to go to hell? No matter what happens in your life, your mother is going to be there when no one else is there. No matter what you do. You can kill someone and your mother's going to be there. I see it all the time in prison. Wives leave. Girlfriends don't come to visit anymore. Fathers lose interest. It's only the mothers that come and visit every week, that send the package."

Kyle replies that he did not mean to cause his mother pain, but he is unhappy living where he lives. He understands his mother moved to keep him off the streets of Philadelphia, but he feels isolated living in a town where he knows no one, where he does not like anybody and nobody seems to like him. He misses his friends. At least hanging out with the bad guys in his town gives him a sense of excitement.

Hakeem is sympathetic but firm. He points out to Kyle that his life is doomed to end in disaster unless he changes course. Hakeem offers to help, to be available for him whenever he wants to talk.

"One year later, the struggle is still going on," Hakeem explains. "Kyle hasn't run off to Philadelphia. He's going to school more often. I tracked down an athletic program that the community started and they agreed to accept him. His mother says that if he keeps up the good work, she'll get him a car. I'm against that. If she's going to allow him to get a car, he should work to pay for part of it. I've been talking to him about getting a job after school and he's promised to try. It's still touch and go. It will be for a while yet. There's no easy solutions. He's a good kid, but I'm sure that if his mother hadn't called the Lifers' Group, Kyle would be in jail now—or dead. You could see it in his face."

Some of the young people whom the lifers help, they never meet personally. Seven days a week, the lifers staff their office, which is in a separate area of the prison. Calls come in from teenagers and parents from around the country and community groups and schools wanting tours and appointments. Sometimes a call may come from a desperate teenager about to commit a crime or suicide. "We had a situation where a guy was in a house planning a stickup and he turned on the TV and *Scared Straight* was on," Qahhar Saahir, treasurer of the Lifers' Group, remembers. "He called in to say that after watching the movie, he decided not to do the stickup." Saahir recalls the dramatic first day he had been assigned to answer the telephones. "I had just been accepted in the group and I was alone in the office. This phone call came in from a woman who said she had a gun and was going to shoot her employer, that he was a real rotten guy and deserved to die. This was my first call and I didn't know what to do. I just kept her talking until I could get someone to eventually call the police out there. We talked her into unloading the gun and turning it over to the police."

Many teenagers and their parents have written thousands of letters to the Lifers' Group over the years. Pete Sanchez, cochairman of the High School Forum, answers many of them. "The kids usually write because they've seen the film. I answer every letter that comes in. Most of them say how much they liked the program." Pete begins to read excerpts from several letters. "My name is Carmen and *Scared Straight* made me think of how irresponsible I've been and I'm determined to change." Another teenager writes: "You may have ruined your life but you've helped those like myself who could have ruined theirs. I'm touched by what you have done."

"That's not to say that the program doesn't have its critics," Pete points out. "Here's one kid who wrote, 'I think your propaganda stinks. All those kids were so tough and when they went to prison, they shut up. I wouldn't let anyone do that stuff to me.' It's interesting," Pete adds, "that the kid signed the letter and then added a P.S. 'If you want, you can write me.' And I did. I told him that I was glad he had written and that he had an attitude that could lead him to prison if he didn't change it, and that we were here to help him if he wanted."

Hakeem with Jimmy and his mother—they've still got a long way to go.

Many letters that the Lifers' Group receive are filled with cries of despair. Charles Allen, called Imo by his friends, is in correspondence with a desperate young man in New England. "I have just seen your program," the young man writes, "and I thought I'd write to you for help because there is nobody else that can do anything for me. I have done it all—drugs, alcohol, breaking and entering, robbery. I get locked up all the time because I won't obey their rules. They try to give me medication which I won't take and I keep mutilating myself with pencils or whatever I can stick in my arms and have to be restrained and taken to the hospital. I go to programs like Alcoholics Anonymous and drug treatment but they don't do much for me. The doctor says that I don't want to let them help me and I think he is right. I have a two-year sentence right now. Please write. I am a lifer, too. P.S. I am nineteen years old."

Imo replies by pointing out to the writer that he is not a lifer . . . he only has a two-year sentence—and that his whole life is still before him. Imo notes that he seems intelligent, but the problems he has are beyond the ability of the lifers to help him therapeutically. They can only give him support in his efforts to help himself by writing and talking to him on the phone. To encourage him to help himself, Imo tells him that there are men in here with serious problems who have pulled themselves up and that he can do the same if he wants.

And then there are letters of gratitude. This one was written about lifer Gary Davis:

"I was heartbroken that one of my children would take the wrong road in life. Every night I would wonder if she were dead or alive, was she abused, raped, or lying in the street somewhere freezing to death or selling her body for another fix. Was she killed by someone, dismembered and never to be found or heard from again? I was sick, scared, worried, and couldn't sleep at night. Through it all, Gary consoled me, encouraged me, and sympathized with me. He kept calling and writing and helped make me strong through this ordeal. I'm happy to say that after three months away from home, my daughter's back and in counseling and has a job . . . She's struggling and at times depressed . . . but she too talks to Gary to whom she can admit a lot of things that she can't tell us. And we're proud of her. Gary is very sensitive toward people, he can relate to their suffering, he can feel their pain, cause he has felt it . . .''

Despairing parents wrote to Chris DeLuise ("Crazy Chris") about their son:

"After months and months of talking to countless doctors and trying different programs, feeling we were getting no help and getting nowhere, the phone call to your organization gave us our first relief. For the first time we felt that we had someone who could relate to how we were feeling and understand the desperation we were experiencing . . . Talking to you now on a regular basis has helped us more than you know. You made sense, you didn't just criticize. You made us realize that bailing him out all the time was not helping him. Joseph is now in a drug program and is now doing it on his own. He is still having his ups and downs, but thank God he is better than before."

But for all the families they are able to help, there are many young people who come into contact with the Juvenile Awareness Program that the Lifers' Group will not reach.

Tariq Commander, once a college student, editor of the campus newspaper, and civil rights activist, is deeply aware of the limitations they face. "First of all," he says, "we don't get to see the kids on a regular basis. They come here one time and then maybe they'll visit once or twice more. If their parents allow it, they will write to us or call us and we will write to them or call them. We have to be careful there, because we do not consider ourselves role models. The reason we are in here is because we are losers and we don't want the children to identify with that.

"Then we have the problem of the type of kid that comes in here today. Kids like Ernie, who are making big money on the streets dealing drugs. I can't stop a child like that from selling drugs if he's making good money. It's impossible for us to tell a child to get a minimum wage job when he's making fifteen hundred dollars a week. We can fool ourselves if we think we can offer something that will turn a child like that around. That doesn't mean we don't try. We do make it clear to him that sooner or later he's going to wind up in here and have everything taken away from him. But it's hard to get a fifteen-year-old kid to see that.

"I try to emphasize that a lot of times kids feel that they're locked into selling drugs, that it's the only way they can make it. I try to show them the relationship between the drug dealer and store owner . . . they're getting their product, they're packing their product, they're giving credit—just like the store owner. I tell them that the only thing is that you never thought you had the ability to run a store. But in selling drugs, you got the exact same entrepreneurial skills.

"We are more effective with kids who don't feel they're

worth anything. We can help them change if they want to, but we can't make them change. They have to want to change themselves."

Willie Allen, who tried to break through to Ernie and did not succeed, adds: "What is important is that in spite of all these limitations, there are kids we do save. We know that. We have proof of that. How many, I don't think anybody really knows. We know there are hundreds, probably thousands of kids who have told us that we have played an important role in helping them change their lives. How many more there are that haven't told us, I don't know. Maybe there are more of them than the others."

College students—some may be our future prosecutors, judges, police, or corrections officers.

THE FORUMS

CHAPTER 7

The college students have entered the main building and are visibly nervous. Prison is a place that evokes their worst nightmares and to be inside a maximum security penitentiary for the first time in their lives causes them anxiety.

While college students have visited East Jersey State Prison for a number of years, the tour was originally conducted by prison officials who did not permit the students to talk with the prisoners. When the Lifers' Group took over the program, the format was changed to a forum, to allow a dialogue between the prisoners and the students. In 1988 the program was expanded to include high schools.

From the lifers' point of view, the forums give them the opportunity to express their viewpoint about the criminal justice system, prison, parole, probation, and long sentences. The students visit for many reasons. Some plan to be future prosecutors, judges, police, or corrections officers. A few hope that the lifers may provide solutions to personal problems, such as delinquency and drug or alcohol abuse. And others are just curious about prison life.

In the forum the students sit in the auditorium while the lifers sit facing them, below the stage. The discussion is informal and the students are free to ask any questions they want.

Mike Ayala and Pete Sanchez are the respective chairmen of the college and high school forums. Today there is a college forum—a sophomore criminal justice class from a nearby university. Mike Ayala and Pete Sanchez introduce themselves to the students and then ask if they have any questions. After a few moments of awkward silence, a young woman asks somewhat loudly and nervously what Mike Ayala has done.

"My crime is homicide," he replies, quite candidly.

Before the discussion continues, Bilal Abdul-Aziz diplomatically interrupts. "While every one of us is willing to answer questions about their crime," he says, "perhaps it would be more fruitful to begin the session by answering questions relating more directly to prison life before we get into what got us here. In that way, you can get to know us a little before you ask personal questions." Underlying this response is Aziz's concern that the students may become more involved in the sensational aspects of crime and ignore the more important issues.

Mark, a student who tends to regard the lifers skeptically, asks why the prisoners are allowed to dress in street clothes and have television sets and stereos in their cells. Pete Sanchez asks the group what they think the answer is. Elise, who is sympathetic to the prisoners, answers, "To make it comfortable for you, so you won't riot." "Right," Pete Sanchez replies. "Television sets are a means of pacification. It keeps our minds distracted from the things that we need to do for ourselves. We have guys in here who should be reading books instead of watching television or playing basketball in the yard. A man can stay in bed all day long and watch soaps or listen to music or play ball. Physically he can be strong as a bull, but very weak upstairs." Pete begins to elaborate on a theme that all the lifers support—mandatory education. "If we were running the prison, we would make education a requirement for all prisoners. Like at Leavenworth, if you don't have an education when you come into prison, you got to get one—or else you stay in lockup twenty-three hours a day. Guys shouldn't be allowed to have television, contact visits, food packages if they don't get an education."

Willie Allen addresses the question of clothing. "By letting us wear our own clothing, it saves the state money. The state's supposed to clothe a man every six months, even though it's only two pairs of khaki pants, a work shirt, boots, and so on. By allowing a man's family to clothe him, the state doesn't have to supply him."

Another student asks if the state gives them television sets and stereos. Tony Hayes laughingly replies, "We have to buy them ourselves. Some of us may have families who buy them for us. Others pay for it out of the money they earn in the prison. Whatever we buy has to come directly from the store in its original packaging so that nothing is smuggled inside the appliance, such as drugs or weapons."

The question of how men earn money in prison is raised. "Like it says in the television commercial," Mike Ayala, answers. "We make money the old-fashioned way, we earn it." Mike begins to spell out the variety of jobs performed by prisoners: cooking; serving and preparing food; cleaning up in the kitchen or the mess halls; helping the sick; making clothes, mattresses, and signs; fixing electrical and plumbing equipment; painting and constructing facilities; and clerking the general or law library, the commissary, and storage areas. "The pay scale varies from about a dollar and a half to about six dollars a day, depending on the job," Mike concludes.

A young woman rises to correct him. "You mean an hour, not a day!" The lifers laugh. Willie Allen forcefully answers. "We mean a day, young lady! Prison is a slave plantation! Last week one of the guards showed me his paycheck for two weeks, including overtime. Eighteen hundred dollars! Eighteen hundred dollars for two weeks and he don't do noth-

Abdul-Aziz describes prison . . .

ing but turn the key. I worked like a dog for two weeks. You know how much I made? Twenty-five dollars. That's right, twenty-five dollars. Wake up, sister!"

The conversation turns to the living conditions inside prison. The students want to know what the food is like. What are the medical conditions? The lifers explain that while the food is nourishing it is usually tasteless and poorly prepared. Some men, in fact, do not eat prison food but depend upon food packages that friends or relatives bring or send. A prisoner is allowed up to sixty pounds of food a month, more than enough for three meals a day.

to a college student sitting among lifers.

As for medical conditions, most of the men feel that they are fine—"as long as you don't get sick." Several men tell how they or others had to wait for days to see a doctor when they were ill, were given aspirin for serious illnesses, and were misdiagnosed by doctors they considered to be inadequate. One of the men was asked about AIDS patients and was told that while there were a number of men with AIDS in prison, the really sick cases were transferred to a special hospital to die.

The students then raise the question of why prisons are so overcrowded. The answer: "More drugs, higher crime rates, and stiffer laws." Nelson Guzman explains: "Under the old law, which was known as 2A, under which many of us were sentenced, when a man received a life sentence he was eligible for parole after fourteen years, eight months. Or if a man was sentenced from five to ten years, he would be eligible for parole let's say in three years. But then the public began to think that we weren't serving enough time, so they cried out for tougher sentences. And the politicians responded with 2C, which sets a mandatory minimum sentence. That means if you get a life sentence you have to serve twenty-five years before you're even eligible for parole. So guys serve more time instead, which means that there are fewer vacancies and the prison gets overcrowded."

"Does overcrowding lead to violence?" "No question about that," Pete Sanchez replies. "Prison is a violent enough place to begin with and when you keep shoveling people in one end and not taking them out the other, something's got to give." Willie Allen picks up on this. "You know why prison is the politest place in the world? Why everybody says 'excuse me'? Why everybody goes out of their way to be courteous to another? Because you know that the next man can be as dangerous as you."

One of the students asks Mike Ayala, because of his small size, if a little man gets picked on in prison. Mike responds by pointing out that size has less to do with getting abused than the way you carry yourself. "Before my homicide, I had never been to prison. I believed that I was going to be eaten up alive. I said to myself, 'They're going to try and abuse you mentally and physically.' I was scared. I was smaller than most guys here. My knees was knocking. I was shaking. So the first thing I did was to take a metal spoon they gave me and sharpen it into a weapon. This is one of the things that my friends in the county jail taught me. I rubbed it on the concrete with some water, I scraped it back and forth, back and forth, back and forth, little by little, until my hands were raw. Fortunately, there was some tape on the wall of my cell. I wrapped it in tape so that it couldn't be seen. I was ready to use it. I swore that the first individual that would try to take anything from me, my food or me, I was going to make him the example. I had fifteen years to pull and I was damned if I would let anybody abuse me. Nobody was going to disrespect me. When I went to the shower by myself and couldn't take the spoon, I had a custom to take a razor and stick it on my tongue. Anything could happen in that kind of a situation and I didn't want to leave myself vulnerable. There might only be one officer around and he could be at the other end of the tier. You could kill someone and no one would never know who did it. Without going into the details, let's just say, only once did I have to give a guy a close shave. What

A student learns some unpleasant truths about "rehabilitation" ...

makes the difference is the way you carry yourself in here. Size is less important."

Mark wants to know why there are so many black people in jail. Abdul-Aziz gives him an answer. "Because of the inequality in our system, we're driven down certain roads. The pimp, the numbers runner, the robber, the drug dealer. They're the people who have always had the semblance of having made it. We have high unemployment. Our households are run by women. There is no family structure. We are confined to a certain geographical location in our community. Our education is nil. What they were teaching me didn't apply

from Lifers' Vice-President Maxwell Melvins.

to me. I was into drugs, into guns. We don't manufacture them, but they're in our community."

Mark persists. "What about the people you killed?" "Nobody is saying that we should not be punished for things that we did," Abdul-Aziz replies. "And most of us are sorry for what we did. We can't tell you how sorry we are. It was wrong. But also remember we live in a society in which people kill every day. The President of the United States goes into any country he wants and kills a few hundred people because he doesn't like the government. And nobody puts him in prison. We don't object to paying for our crimes. We do object to those people who are self-righteous and say you did this, you did that."

Mark is not convinced. "What if the guy has committed a crime against you or a member of your family," he asks with a certain amount of anger in his voice. The lifers sense that he may be talking from personal experience. Tony Hayes, a soft-spoken, extremely articulate man, answers the question. "It depends on the circumstances. I may want revenge personally and want to see him severely punished or killed. But you can't run a system that way. You have to have some kind of standards. Why did he commit the crime? Was it because of drugs? Why was the man an addict? What opportunities did he have when he was growing up? All these should be considered so he can be given the help he needs."

"If a man commits a really horrible crime, should he be let out of prison?" Elise asks.

"If he's served his punitive time and is not going to commit that crime again—or any crime—why not? What good does it do to keep punishing him when he's already paid the price for what he did?" Pete Foster asks. "Why should you want to keep him in prison any longer?" Mark is quick to answer. "Because you read about men who have been released from prison and commit crimes again. It happens all the time."

"Yes, it does happen," John Chaney responds. "If a man spends, say, fifteen years in prison, learns nothing, is not prepared to return to society, is given seventy-five dollars and turned free, how do you expect him not to return to crime? The state says it spends twenty thousand dollars a prisoner to keep us here. We think it's closer to thirty thousand dollars.

Whatever it is, don't think that the money is being spent on our rehabilitation. It isn't. Most of it is spent on officers' salaries. There are some guards here who make between seventy-five and a hundred thousand dollars a year when you figure in overtime. And some of them only have a high school education."

Elise, visibly disturbed, suddenly stands up. "I'm really upset to hear this. I thought you were learning something. I didn't know you were wasting away. I thought that at least some of you were being rehabilitated." "Rehabilitation doesn't exist in prison," Pete Foster replies. "It doesn't. I'm not saying men don't change themselves in here. They do. But the system isn't geared to that. It doesn't provide adequate counseling. There's only one psychologist for over twenty-two hundred men. So nobody gets individual therapy." Dawud Abdul-Wasi points out, "I don't want to be rehabilitated. Rehabilitation means to restore you to your former state. None of us want to be restored to our former state as a criminal or drug addict. That's the problem with prison. It returns people to the state they were in when they came here."

"Could you have benefited from the Juvenile Awareness Program if you had come in when you were sixteen?" another student asks. Some of the lifers say they went through the program when they were teenagers. "Obviously it didn't help me," one points out. The students laugh. He admits that he was more fascinated by the fact that men were cursing on television than by what was being said. Yet several of the men said they felt they could have benefited had someone taken them in hand as they now try to take others in hand. Willie Allen confesses that even being in the program didn't help him the first time. He was released and came back because he hadn't overcome his drug problem.

Mark uses Willie Allen's confession to resume his attack. "Are you saying then that maybe you can save somebody if they're young enough but that by the time a man reaches this state of incarceration it's too late?" Pete Foster replies. "You've spent almost an hour with us. Tell me, does it seem too late for us? There are a lot of lifers who leave here and go back to society and make it and you never hear about them again. But if one guy should fail, you read about how an 'ex-con' messed up." Dawud Abdul-Wasi reminds the audience, "Many of our outstanding leaders in society spent some time in jail. Nelson Mandela spent twenty-seven years in jail. Malcolm X was an inmate. Gandhi was in prison. Christ was incarcerated before he was executed. If Moses were walking the streets today, he would be an ex-convict." The audience becomes thoughtful.

Pete Sanchez begins the wrap-up of the forum by pointing out to the students, "You're going to be the future lawyers and judges and prosecutors of tomorrow. By knowing what goes on in prisons and seeing that they are run the way they should be, you can do a lot to make prisons turn out productive human beings instead of repeat offenders." Willie Allen calls Mark to the front of the room and seats him between the lifers. Mark is nervous. Willie then asks him a concluding question. "Why do you think they build such high walls around a prison?" Mark replies, "To keep you from escaping." "No!" Willie Allen answers, emphatically. "It's to keep you from seeing in. They don't want you to know what's going on inside these walls. They don't want you to know how your money's being spent. The best thing you can do is what you're doing—to insist on coming here to see what's happening—to make sure that every dollar you spend is being put to the best possible use—to make sure that we are getting the things we need to help us be productive people when we get back on the street."

Mike Ayala asks if there are any other questions. Elise asks the men what they miss the most. Several men immediately reply "sex." The students laugh. Others say "family." "Privacy." "Making a phone call without it being monitored." "Going to the store and buying a soft drink." "Pizza." "I haven't heard a dog bark since 1987." "We don't see squirrels." One man replies, "I miss leaning on a tree."

The forum ends and for several moments the students talk with the lifers in small, informal groups before they leave. Mike is more relaxed in his conversation with the lifers. He later admits that while he has not changed his views about harsh penalties for criminals, he was impressed by the lifers and would think about what they had to say. The young woman who began the session by asking Mike Ayala about his crime no longer openly expresses an interest in what he has done. Later she says to Elise, "To be perfectly honest, I still wanted to know what he did, but it no longer seemed very important. What was important was what he had to say." Elise answers, "I expected to hear men filled with hate and anger. It blew my mind to meet such thoughtful, well-educated, articulate men. It's a shame they had to go to prison to learn this."

Portrait of a life sentence: Calvin Bass, then and now.

TEENAGE LIFERS

CHAPTER 8

In a little over a decade, the average age of prisoners incarcerated at East Jersey State Prison has dropped from twenty-seven to twenty-three. "When I first came to prison, there were very few young guys," Maxwell Melvins, vice-president of the Lifers' Group, recalls. "Now it seems that the young guys outnumber the older guys."

In the 1960s it was relatively rare for a teenager to be sent to prison, even if he committed a violent crime. "In those days you knew if you did something serious, you'd go to a juvenile joint for a few years and be back out on the streets again," Zuberi Bandele recalls. "It was no big deal, unless you did a crime that was pretty heavy and got a lot of publicity." In the 1970s the courts began to impose increasingly heavy sentences on teenagers. Today there are prisoners as young as seventeen at East Jersey State Prison, some of whom will not be released until they are nearly sixty.

For many of them, their life in crime began as children. Often it started with dropping out of school, drinking wine, smoking marijuana, and trying to impress older guys. Then the marijuana became coke or crack, the hooky turned to breaking and entering or armed robbery. "Before you know it, you're packing a gun," Willie Allen points out. "And when you have a gun, someday you'll want to use it. Maybe just for target practice on a roof somewhere. Or to shoot a dog or an animal. But maybe one day you might have to use it to defend yourself against someone else or to keep from getting caught—or maybe, if you're high on crack, you might try it out on a person—because you're angry or you want to see what it's like to shoot somebody." Tony Hayes bears him out. Tony, one of the most thoughtful and articulate men in the prison, came from a strong middle-class family, yet his underlying anger led him, as a high school student, to break and enter into people's homes, until one day he was discovered while committing a burglary and killed the person who caught him.

"On the other hand, there are teenagers in prison who have not committed violent crimes," Zuberi Bandele adds. "People think that you got to be a killer to do a life sentence. Or you got to have committed a number of serious crimes. The system doesn't work that way at all. A lot of guys who are in here are here because they were in the wrong place at the wrong time. I'm not saying they were angels. Some of them were undoubtedly wild. But others were not getting into any serious trouble when they found themselves faced with a homicide charge." He is relaying two of the most important messages that the lifers communicate to the teenagers who they meet: *Seemingly small antisocial acts can have serious unintended consequences.* And, *you don't have to be the one who did the crime to get the sentence. Just being there is enough.*

Some lifers claim they were more victims of circumstances than intent, that they happened to be at the wrong place at the wrong time. "Some kids think it has to be the second, the third, or the fourth time before it happens to you," Rasheed Ali, former vice-president of the Lifers' Group, points out. A good student and athlete in high school who was looking forward to going to college, Rasheed Ali had no trouble with the law. "I was coming home from school, driving, when I picked up my brother and his friend. I dropped them at a store and waited. I had no idea what was going down. They said nothing to me. Suddenly they came running out. It was an armed robbery. A man was shot and killed. They arrested me because someone had taken the license number of my car. I pleaded not guilty. In order to get off, the prosecutor said I had to testify against my brother and his friend. I had to admit that I knew about the robbery and I didn't know about it. My brother and his friend pleaded innocent. So what was I to do? I didn't know the system. I pleaded innocent because I was innocent but my car was involved and the jury found me guilty. The judge hit me hard for not cooperating with the prosecutor against my brother. I got a life sentence and my brother was found guilty of a lesser charge and was out in a few years. I served seventeen years and never hurt anybody."

Charles Helton was sixteen years old when he was arrested. His problem was that of peer pressure, which, according to Superintendent Arvonio, "is the reason why seventy percent of the men are in here today."

"I was not a kid who got in trouble," Helton recalls, "but I was a troubled kid. I'd play hooky from school, smoke reefers, drink alcohol. My parents were seldom home. They each worked, and on different shifts, so that when one was working, the other was sleeping. My mom liked to drink alcohol and smoke marijuana with my friends. She was a pal instead of a mother. That was before she found God and changed her way of life. But I never got into serious trouble until I made a bad choice of friends.

"The big thing in my life was partying. I used to hang out with these two older guys—Bryan and Fred. Bryan was seventeen and Fred eighteen. They liked to drink and party and smoke PCP and so I used to hang out with them and do the same things. My little brother warned me about one of the guys. He thought Bryan would get me in trouble one day. It's too bad I didn't listen.

"One night we were going to this party at the Jersey shore and our car broke down and we had to walk. So when Bryan said, 'Let's steal a car,' we went along with it. We stole this car and we went looking for this party but we never found it. So we're driving along and we're pretty high and we pass a store and Bryan says, 'See that store—let's stick it up.' And he pulls out a gun. Now we didn't need any money. We had about seventy dollars. My parents were middle class and they bought me things when I needed them. So we argued over this and the older guy, Fred, said, 'Okay. I'll stick it up if there are no bullets in the gun.' So Bryan took the bullets out and Fred holds up the store and comes away with about a hundred bucks.

"Now we're driving around and we buy a bag of marijuana from some high school kids but we have no papers and we go to a store to get papers. And Bryan says, 'I'll get the papers.' Fred and I wait for him in the car. The next thing I know I hear this pop and it sounds like a gun and I start the car to get out of there and Bryan comes running out and hops in the car and says. 'I just shot a guy.' As I look back on it now, I think Bryan wanted to shoot somebody all along. He threatened to kill us if we said anything about it to anyone.

"So we drive off and we burn the car and I go to my girlfriend's house. And we don't get caught. About a year later, it's eleven-thirty at night. I'm sleeping and suddenly there's a knock at the door and my mom answers it and there are about ten cops outside. Bryan had told his girlfriend what we did and when he split up with her she was so mad she went and told the cops. And that's how we got busted."

Charles Helton at age 16, sentenced to life plus twelve years.

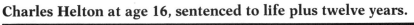

Offered a chance to plea-bargain for a thirty-year term, Charles and his family decided to go to trial. Bryan had confessed to the killing. Charles admitted to charges of robbery and car theft but maintained that he did not know Bryan had intended to hold up the second store, let alone kill anyone—or that the gun he had was loaded. The jury did not believe him. Found guilty of homicide, Charles was sentenced to life in prison, plus an additional twelve to eighteen years for the robberies, car theft, and arson. He was sixteen years old. This means that he would have to serve at least twenty years before he could be considered eligible for parole.

"One thing I vowed was not to let prison break my spirit," Charles said. "I could have been bitter. I could have gone crazy inside, but I didn't. I really tried to take advantage of the programs they had here. I learned a trade. I got myself a high school diploma. I like to work with kids and help keep them out of jail. If I'm lucky, I'll only be in my late thirties when I get out. I'll still be young enough to do something with my life."

Calvin Bass was only fourteen years old when he received a life sentence with a thirty-year stipulation, which means that he will not be eligible for parole until he is forty-four and will probably not be released until he is fifty.

"I was more of an example," says Calvin. "You know how they experiment with rabbits to see what they can do. I was like the rabbit. The judge was saying 'He's fourteen, let's see how much we can give him.' When the judge gave me thirty years, he said, 'Now I want you all on the street to hear what I'm saying and look what's being done.' I buckled.

I got weak in the legs and I sat back down. When he said it, I thought he was saying, 'You're finished. Your life is washed up.' But it still didn't dawn on me really. I thought maybe he was trying to scare me. I was only a kid. But a year after, when my appeals started coming back, I began to realize it was for real.

"Until then, I had done no crimes against people. I had done juvenile offenses. Stolen cars, robbery. I was going with what I'd seen. I admired the style of the guys who had nice clothes, big cars, pretty women, guns, money. That was something I always admired. That was the style. That was what was going down. I wanted to get it. I was going to take it.

"My mother, she knew. She said, I'm telling you don't do this, don't do that, don't do this. She was foreseeing something 'cause she's dealing with experience—and wisdom—'cause wisdom comes from experience. I listened to her, but something else was on my mind. When I left the house, I left what she said behind me.

"When I talk to the juveniles on the stage, I don't cut no corners. I tell them that the system ain't right and what they're doing ain't right. You're messing up all a way around. There's no justice in the system. So when you're messing around, they're just gonna finish you off. You start out playing with cigarettes, cut school, smoke reefer in the alleyway. Then you move up. Everybody falls into it. Black kids, white kids, oriental kids. It's not a racial thing. They say, 'The only thing I do is steal a car. The only thing I do is smoke reefer.' They don't understand they got a bad attitude and a bad attitude can lead to a murder. A guy disrespects you, you don't give a damn about, you will kill him, because you don't really care.

Even if you're scared, your pride is so big that you stand up and do it. I had the same attitude problem, the same wrong outlook on life.

"When I tell them I got to do thirty years, they get shocked. They say, 'I could never deal with that. I'd kill myself.' I tell 'em no, I ain't giving up and I ain't never gonna give up on my life. I had to start learning. If I ain't well educated, I'm gonna be left behind with the uneducated people. I don't want to be around them no longer. I see fools, I don't care what they have. If they don't have the proper perspective, wanting to help things, build things, create things, change things, I don't want to have no dealings with them. I made a wrong choice. When I needed help, I couldn't ask anyone. I wasn't strong enough.

"Lot of people in here hold strong solutions to society's problems because they ain't in it no more. A coach can call certain plays because he once played football but doesn't play anymore. Only a few are blessed to call it as they see it. Now I can call it as I see it because I know how the game's supposed to be."

For many teenagers with long sentences, reality sets in slowly. At first they act in prison as if they were still on the outside. Rather than work or go to school, they hang out with their friends, play basketball, watch television, take drugs, and get into fights. When older guys try to counsel or help them, they do not listen.

"When I came to prison," Maxwell Melvins recalls, "I was just like them. You couldn't tell me nothing. I was really wild. But there were many older guys who would help out young kids like myself. They would push books on them, get them to get an education, take religion seriously, and keep in contact with their families. They would also protect you from other guys who might prey on you and try to take something from you, your possessions or your manhood.

"Today there are so many young people in jail that it's not the same. Many guys don't want to hear about school and stuff like that. At least, not now, not in the beginning. But sooner or later they'll settle down. That's one of the things the Lifers' Group is working on now—to have a program for juvenile offenders in prison. Some of the kids have already asked for it. With so many kids coming into the system with such long bids, I'm afraid we're going to be busy for years to come."

A well-kept secret—weapons made by prisoners.

VIOLENCE

On New Year's Eve, in the shower room in Four Wing, two prisoners argued over a cup. The man who held the cup found it and claimed it was his because he now had it. The other man claimed he left it on the dining room table and it belonged to him. "I ain't giving you nothing, how 'bout that?" the man who held the cup said. The other prisoner said nothing, but became very quiet. Quickly he returned to his cell, removed a knife he had hidden behind the toilet, and returned to the shower. Two quick thrusts and it was over. A man lay dead on the floor with the disputed cup gripped firmly in his hand.

Joey Mackiewicz remembers his first encounter with violence in prison. "The first day I was here, I was in the dining room eating lunch and a guy comes up behind me and throws hot coffee right in the face of the guy sitting opposite me. The first day! Over nothing. It blew my mind! And I had to keep on eating as if nothing had happened. You mind your own business if you want to survive in prison."

Prison is "macho" society carried to its extreme. It's like a Western town in which everybody waits to see who's going to draw first. The tougher you are physically, the more respect you get.

"Some men come into prison ready to make their reputations," Rasheed Ali notes. "There are guys who spend their whole life in prison just because they made a reputation as being bad. And every time they did something, the judge just added more years to their sentence. There's always the new guy, what we call a "fish," that comes in here thinking he's going to have to make his bones. He has that mentality that says, 'I want to flex my muscles a little bit, I can start some stuff, I can go for bad now. I want guys to see that I'm tough.' "

One of the unwritten rules in prison is don't threaten someone unless you are prepared to back it up immediately. "When you threaten somebody, you invite them to cut your throat," Pete Sanchez notes. "A guy might not fight you head on. Maybe I'm not as good as you are. I can't fight you like that 'cause I'm gonna lose. So I'll try to get even. I'll get something that will make me equal to you. A pipe, getting a 'shiv' and stabbing him. In the yard not too long ago, this is exactly what happened. One guy was arguing with another and told him 'to come on with it.' Immediately the guy he threatened went and got his brother and a 'shank,' and the two of them walked up to the guy who made the threat as he was lifting weights. The guy saw them coming and he grabbed two twenty-pound weights, one in each hand, to punch them with. The brothers began to cut him and when they saw that they wasn't doing much with the shank, they started to beat him over the head with weights. The guy kept defending himself by beating on them with the weights he was holding. When the police finally broke it up, the guy who was attacked beat his chest as blood poured down his face from a head wound and cried out proudly for everyone in the yard to hear, 'See, you punks can't kill me. I'm still standing.' Blood pouring down his face as he's saying this. Big 'macho' man! Crazy! Real prison mentality."

Sometimes violence erupts without warning. A man walks into a mess hall and accidentally bumps someone, or someone in the yard glances at a person the wrong way. "There are people in the prison who aren't playing with a full deck, who are crazy, who will stab you and you will never know why. Even they don't know why," Mike Ayala says. "The only time you feel completely safe is at night when they double-lock the door to your cell."

For a young prisoner coming into jail for the first time, prison is a terrifying experience. "Every one of us is scared," Willie Allen recalls. "No matter how big you are. You're trembling inside, but you can't show it. And when you have your first encounter, you have to go all out to beat the guy and make sure everybody knows about it, officers and prisoners. You want to establish a reputation as being someone wild and crazy, because in prison, people don't mess with a crazy man."

Rasheed Ali remembers his first day: "Your heart beats faster. Guys are looking down at you from their cells. They call out to you. These people are killers. They killed ten people, you think. They can do that to their mothers, their kid brothers, their loved ones. Imagine what they will do to you. You say, I can protect myself, but these guys are experienced.

This is their home. They're relaxed here. If you survive the physical part, how will you stand up mentally? I had to prepare myself to do whatever I had to do. If they come to hurt me, or do some bodily harm to me, that meant I have to be prepared to do something to them before they did it to me. My attitude was not to come to jail to get a reputation. I always had a dream to go home."

Maxwell Melvins recalls how every man is tested when he comes to prison: "A guy sees you have something he wants and comes up to you and says, 'I'm gonna take that from you. What are you going to do about it?' He tries to belittle you amongst the prisoners that are there by taking your stuff. So I tell him, 'You ain't gonna take nothing from me!' Then you

When pent-up frustrations are unleashed—corrections officers in riot gear.

fight. But I learned quickly, you don't fight anyone fair. There's no such thing as a fair fight in prison. Couple times I fought, the guy had a pipe. So I had to get something to defend myself with."

The most feared form of violence in jail is sexual violence. Harvey George remembers his first encounter with that threat: "I was really devastated the first time I was locked up. I was scared. I had heard all sorts of stories about what guys will do to you. There was a guy by the name of Henry. He used to come in and give me candy and pies and stuff. I thought he was just being nice. Then one Sunday morning, he told me 'Stay back in your cell this morning.' I said, 'For what?' He said, 'Look, punk! You know what this is. I didn't give you those pies and all just because I'm your mama. Stay back in your cell!' I was like trembling. I was a country boy and I didn't understand those things. I thought, what did I get myself into? So I told one of the guys I knew and he said 'Man, kill that sucker.' So he got me a razor blade. He said, 'When the doors open, don't say nothing, but go right to his cell and kill him.' I was so struck with fear that when the doors opened, I couldn't move. The guy then came into my cell and he hit me right in the face—Boom! And I was so angry that I began cutting into him. I cut into his face, his chest, everywhere. Fear was making me do that. I was shaking with fear. And anger. He seemed like such a good guy. He was nice to me. I really didn't expect that.

"You have to be prepared to kill when you come in here," Harvey continues. "You definitely have to. If a guy don't take you sexually, he'll take your manhood in a thousand different ways. A guy can put you under his wing to protect you from other guys. You'll be known as a man who can't take care of yourself. You'll need another man to take care of you. Guys travel on this. When I went to reformatory, I was scared. So I was going to let them know that I was tough. I got into a fight in the reception area. I went there ready. A guy said something to me, I went right after him. He made a remark before he got the words out of his mouth, *Bam!* I'd hit him. You couldn't say nothing to me. If it even sounded like you was saying something I didn't like, I'd knock you down. I'd hit your head. I was surviving. I had made up in my mind I was going to survive. From that day on."

"Trenton was intense! Trenton was intense! It was the worst prison I've ever seen. If you're weak, you don't have a chance. I had to make up my mind that I was going to be ready for things—that nobody's going to say nothing to me about sex or I'll kill you. That was my mentality. If a guy's not ready to do that, the guys will see his fear. They smell it, they see it, they hunt guys down and get them. A guy like me, they see that 'hey, he's ready to die. He's a fool, don't mess with him.' They knew my attitude was 'yeah, let's die.' "

For the man who is afraid of becoming a victim of somebody else's rage or who fears sexual abuse, he can request to be removed from the general population and placed in protective custody. The administration calls it "p.c." The men inside refer to it as "punk city." A man in p.c. is confined to his cell twenty-three hours a day and is allowed out for recreation in a special yard. Most prisoners have contempt for any man who seeks refuge there.

Not all men in protective custody are there because they want to be. If the administration learns through an informer that a man is targeted for violence, they will automatically place him in p.c. until they can send him to another prison. This system provides prisoners with a chance to get rid of somebody they don't like. If a man is dealing in drugs and has a rival, or owes somebody money he can't pay back, all he needs to do is anonymously inform the authorities that someone's life is in danger and they will remove him.

The violence that is perhaps most feared by both prisoners and officers alike is a prison riot. The pent-up frustrations of thousands of men can be suddenly unleashed, often with terrifying results. In the 1960s and 70s prisons throughout America erupted in riots, often as a result of the harsh and often inhuman conditions of prison life. It was a time when the country was undergoing social and political upheavals. In the South African-Americans were struggling for civil rights. On the streets of the cities, hundreds of thousands of people were protesting against the war in Vietnam. These struggles had their counterparts in prisons from Attica in New York to Soledad in California. In 1974 Trenton State Prison erupted and Charles Allen, known as "Imo" to his friends, a member of the Lifers' Group and chairman of the Prisoner's Representative Committee, was caught in the middle:

"It was a time when prisoners were being placed in the hole—solitary confinement—for their political ideas. Any considered to be a radical could be confined for long periods of time for what they thought rather than what they did. In 1975, in Trenton prison, there was an alleged escape attempt in solitary. Weapons had been smuggled into the prison. I was very young, just nineteen. I didn't believe what I was seeing. I was in solitary when it happened. I found myself in the middle

Charles "Imo" Allen, advocate of prisoners' rights, meets with Superintendent Patrick Arvonio.

of a shootout between prisoners against state troopers and prison guards. I saw two officers get shot. A guy I happened to know was gunned down in front of me. He was a guy who tried to give younger fellows like myself a sense of direction. He was shot forty times. He was laying right next to my cell. The officers had machine guns. I knew he was dead from all the holes. I had to count them because the other guys wanted to know how many holes he had in him. Another individual was coming down the tier with his hands on his head. He called out, 'I'm not in this.' Before he got halfway down the tier, the police shot him down. They tried to shoot him in the head but hit his upraised arms. He saved his life by playing dead. That was the awakening in my life of how serious prison was—and led me to get into representative work."

Imo Allen became an advocate of prisoners' rights, mediating the grievances of prisoners to the administration. Shortly after he was transferred to East Jersey State Prison, a crisis developed that he was called upon to negotiate. "An intense situation developed when there was a food strike in one wing of the prison. The wing representative had been locked up for inciting to riot, which he vehemently denied doing. The men demanded he be released and refused to work. The situation was tense. Any moment a riot could break out in the whole prison. There was a threat of bringing in state troopers or the national guard. The warden was on vacation. I got on the phone and talked with him and offered a compromise. I said that if I could convince the men in the striking wing to return to work, would he let the representative out on his return. The warden agreed. I then talked things over with a committee from the striking men. After hours of intense negotiation, they reluctantly agreed. The strike ended. The wing representative was let out the next day and an internal investigation revealed that he was not guilty of the charges against him. The food also improved."

Perhaps the greatest tension that exists within a prison is between the prison guards and the prisoners. Generally there is no love lost between the two, although there are many examples of friendships that develop between individual prisoners and guards. Every day there are many minor conflicts between the men inside and the men who guard them. Rarely are these confrontations physical. Mostly they are verbal and if the prisoner does not respond in what the guard feels to be a proper manner, he can be written up on charges. There are eighty violations in the prison for which a man may be written up, ranging from fighting and possession of drugs to being in the wrong place without a pass.

Drugs are a serious problem at East Jersey State Prison, as they are in almost every prison. As Reverend King Webster, who once used and sold drugs in prison, observes, "Having drugs here is like gold. It's like water in the desert." "I can understand why men take drugs in prison," comments Director of Operations Steve Maggi, whose major responsibility is the discovery of narcotics within the prison. "The life in here is so boring, almost everybody gets high. It's inherent in the nature of prison."

Steve Maggi's effectiveness is based on a network of informants who supply him with information about what is happening throughout the prison. "You can't plan a mass disturbance without my knowing about it. My informants are so varied, I know what's happening in every area of the prison.

They can trust me. I have a reputation as being a superhero and I do nothing to discourage it. There isn't a drug bust that goes down that I'm not in on. I find most of the weapons, I help with the investigations when something goes wrong. A guy has to be involved in the activity to be an informant. A guy who isn't close to the activity can't be an informant. But I make a point of telling them that if they turn up dirty, they're gonna buy like everybody else. I've busted informants if they're not clean.

"The main reason we have drugs in here is because of contact visits. Outsiders bring it in. The only way to stop that from happening is to limit physical contact between prisoners and their families. The result would be that we would make the many suffer for the few. And the tensions inside this place would rise to a boiling point. So we do the next best thing. We try to catch narcotics after it enters the prison.

"Every time you open a door, you don't know if a guy's got a weapon, how he's going to react. If he's got a large amount of narcotics, he knows he's going to do a lot of 'ad seg' time [time locked in solitary]. So why not get a piece of the officer that's coming to get him?

"Guys know that I'm extremely fair. I'll never set a guy up. If a guy has a small amount of marijuana, I won't choke it out of him. If he's swallowed a large amount, I'll get him to a hospital, right away. I play the game straight up. If he gets rid of it, I don't pursue. I'm looking for the big distributors, not the small users. I'll bust them if I catch them, but I'm not out to harass a guy for the sake of a few joints."

When a man is caught with narcotics or charged with violating a prison rule, such as being in an unauthorized area without a pass, he is taken to Courtline, where his case is decided by a hearing officer who will judge the case. While most men are willing to accept the consequences of being caught doing something that is substantively in violation of the rules, they resent officers who use charges to run their wings. Many times, prisoners are brought before Courtline on charges that may be within the letter of the administrative code, but are, in the opinion of one experienced officer, "Mickey Mouse charges by inexperienced or incompetent officers, who don't know how to deal with the men."

Courtline hearings are strictly administrative and convictions cannot be used in a court of law, nor can they directly increase the time a prisoner serves. However, the hearing officer can indirectly add to the time a man serves by taking away from him the good time he has earned toward reducing his sentence. The hearing officer can also punish a prisoner by suspending his visiting, commissary, or other privileges or by placing the offender in solitary confinement or administrative segregation. The verdict can be overruled or punishment reduced by the superintendent, and a prisoner can also earn back some of the time he has lost.

The harshest punishment that can be handed down in a Courtline hearing is sentencing a man to the "hole" (solitary confinement) or administrative segregation, known as "ad seg." Both are isolation units. A prisoner in solitary confinement is confined to his cell during the length of his sentence and is not allowed any visits or recreation. Every three days he is allowed out to take a shower. However, no one can be kept in solitary for more than thirty consecutive days. If a man is sentenced to spend more than thirty days, he must be

A prisoner locked in solitary confinement for breaking a prison rule.

allowed out for a short period of time into the general population before he returns to solitary to finish his sentence.

Administrative segregation ("ad seg") differs from solitary in that a man can be kept in isolation as long as a year for each offense he has committed in prison. Men who have been convicted of multiple sentences or are considered dangerous by the administration may spend years in administrative segregation. When a man is moved from one place to another, he is chained hand and foot from the time he leaves his cell until he arrives at his destination. If the prisoner is considered violent, the transfer is videotaped in order to show that he was not abused by the officers, or if restraint was necessary, that it was not excessive. Because of the length of the sentence, men in "ad seg" are allowed out for recreation approximately eight hours a week and can have limited noncontact visits and phone privileges.

At one time a man could be put in solitary confinement without a hearing. He was placed in an extremely small room, often without heat or light, with only a bed and a mattress that he received only at night. He was fed bread and water at least twice a day and often beaten. He was not allowed to write or read anything except the Bible. Today the solitary rooms at East Jersey State Prison are furnished and have television, and a prisoner is allowed reading and writing materials. The food is the same food served to the rest of the prisoners and beatings are almost nonexistent. But while there have been improvements in material comforts, the isolation that a man suffers as a result of being locked up takes a psychological toll on many men.

"For some men," Harvey George points out, "the hole is

a nightmare. It's not the physical treatment. People don't get arbitrarily beaten up like they used to. It's the psychological beating that's hard for many guys. Some men go crazy being locked up all alone with nobody to talk to for hours. It's not as bad today as it used to be. They have recreation where guys can get into a yard, play ball, and talk. But it's still a lot of time spent inside by yourself. And every time you're taken out of your cell, you're made to strip, you're handcuffed and chained. It's really rubbed into your nose that you've been a bad boy."

A Courtline hearing officer may listen to as many as ten cases a day. Often the charges are minor, as was the case of Charles O'Rourke, accused of refusing to go to work. The years in prison have worn O'Rourke down, like water running over a stone. He pleads guilty but explains with difficulty that he was depressed and anxious because he was waiting for a letter from the parole board that was long overdue. The infraction is a minor one and the hearing officer gives him a suspended sentence of loss of privileges. Another prisoner, who refused to go to work because he had the flu, is found guilty and receives a thirty-day loss of privileges, suspended for sixty days. Although this means that he will not actually be punished, he is angry and stalks out of the room. He feels his sentence is unjust because he was too ill to work and the charge was unfair. No one has a greater passion for justice than a man in jail.

While prisoners are cynical about getting justice in a Courtline hearing, investigating and disciplinary officers, as well as the hearing officer, try to be impartial and a number of cases are either dismissed or overruled by Superintendent Arvonio. An example is the case of Calvin Bass, a member of the

Lifers' Group, who was charged with planning an escape. The case began with a letter that was allegedly sent by Bass and returned to the prison because it seemingly had been sent to the wrong address. The envelope was opened by prison officials to determine who had sent it. Inside was a plan for an escape in the form of a letter that was signed with Calvin Bass's name. Based on the letter, Bass was charged with planning an escape and immediately locked up in solitary. The investigating officer, Sergeant Randy Sandkuhl, interviewed Bass, who strongly maintained he was innocent and offered to take a lie-detector test. Sergeant Sandkuhl's gut feeling was that Bass was telling the truth, although he could find no concrete evidence at the time to prove his innocence.

Bass, handcuffed and in leg chains, was brought into Courtline. The disciplinary officer who was present, Richard Piper, looked at both the letter that was supposed to have been written by Bass and samples of his handwriting from other sources. "It was obvious to me," Piper concluded, "that they were not the same. I felt that someone had it in for Bass and was trying to set him up. It happens all the time in here. Guys try to get each other in trouble, sometimes for no good reason." A handwriting analysis had been ordered from the state police but had not yet been made. The hearing officer, after reviewing the evidence, found Bass not guilty, because she felt there was not sufficient evidence to convict him. However, without a handwriting analysis, she could not definitively conclude that Bass had not written the letter. As a result, prison officials decided to ship Bass out to Trenton State Prison just in case it turned out he was an escape artist. Bass protested against the transfer and argued that it was unjust.

This decision was brought to the attention of Superintendent Arvonio, who was angry that the handwriting analysis had not been done by the state police. After his complaint, the report was on his desk within hours. It confirmed that Bass had not written the letter. The order to transfer Bass was canceled and he was let out of solitary and returned to the general population. While he was given credit for the pay he lost while in lockup and his good time and other privileges were restored, nothing could be done to compensate him for the time he was locked up.

The fact that efforts are made to ensure that prisoners receive due process when they are accused of violating the administrative code helps reduce tension inside a prison. Every perceived injustice can be the spark that triggers a revolt. In the 1960s and 70s revolts and violence increased throughout prisons in America, often as a reaction to the harsh, often inhuman and unjust conditions of prison life and the unwillingness of officials to listen to grievances.

Today, as prisons became increasingly overcrowded, most prison authorities fear there will be increased violence. In every prison there is always a volatile combination of dangerous, often emotionally disturbed men, a large number of weapons, and an unwritten code that encourages men to fight rather than talk when a dispute flares up. Overloading the system increases the pressures on the men inside. This results in an increase of individual cases of violence and can lead to an explosion throughout the entire prison itself. The consequences could be large-scale massacres in which both prisoners and officers would be killed—a tragedy that has already happened many times in prisons in America.

A man must first come to grips with himself—Lifer Goldie Boone begins with the Bible.

TRANSFORMATION

CHAPTER 10

Prison is a place of despair. Most prisoners began life with few, if any, advantages and many disadvantages—homes without parents, money, love, or emotional support and surrounded by every conceivable social disorder. Prison deprives a man of his ability to be productive, to earn a decent wage at a job, have normal relationships with women, to be a father to his children, a husband to his wife, a son to his parents. Men who are immature and have not learned responsibility live in a society in which their lives are regulated and independence is not allowed. Steven Maggi notes, "We treat men like children in here. We don't give a man the opportunity to become an adult. You have to let the leash go further and further until they are on their own. We don't do that in here." For some men, prison is such an environment of hopelessness that they seek to escape through drugs—the abyss into which so many fell in the first place.

"Prison is not a place designed to rehabilitate men," Superintendent Patrick Arvonio states point-blank. "We do not rehabilitate men in here. We do not have the personnel. We can and do provide them with opportunities to better themselves if they want. Though quite frankly, I feel that for most of the men in here, it's too late on this level."

"This is a place without hope," comments Tom Julian, former director of operations. "I sometimes stand in the middle of the dining room during mess hours and watch the men file by and I think how hopeless it is for most of them. The way we rehabilitate men in prison is to make old men of them."

Qahhar Saahir's experience confirms this. "It's killing me—being down like this—it's killing me. It's kicking my butt. It hurts. I always told my mother 'nobody can break me. Ain't got enough time to break me.' Well, they broke me. They made me a believer. My ego ain't that macho thing anymore. You got to pay for doing wrong. It took a life bid to teach me that."

Tony Hayes observes that prison "is a myopic community. Lot of guys are caught up in the past. They're proud of their crimes. The other day a guy boasted about his fifteen thousand dollars worth of watches. His life is wasting away in prison. His life is being taken from him. And he's doing nothing to remedy the situation."

Yet some men do change their lives in prison. They transform themselves through education, religion, counseling, programs like the Lifers' Group, the love of their wives and children, and through their own desire to learn and be better than they were when they came in.

Men serving life terms are often the best candidates to

change their lives. The length of the sentence has a lot to do with it. They have a lot of time on their hands. Yet the first few years they are in prison, many of them rebel against the system. They are young and angry and bitter at the length of their sentence when its impact finally hits them.

Muqtadir Shabazz, who became one of the Lifers' Group photographers, remembers: "When I first came to prison, I was wild. I didn't think I was going to make it for fourteen years. I didn't care what I was doing. I started to go to lockup, ten, fifteen days at a time. I was disrespecting the police, getting locked up all the time. Then older guys would say, read this book, read that book. I started to get an education. I started to read about prison problems, personal problems. Educated guys would say to me, 'write an essay.' I had never written an essay before. How do you write an essay? I had been away from school for years. So I'd write something and they broke it down. They kept me writing, writing, writing until finally I began to feel good about myself. I no longer started worrying that nobody else is gonna care about me. Instead, I started caring about myself. That's what started me seeing the clear open light."

Roland Gebert was seventeen years old when he was sentenced to life in prison for homicide. Son of middle-class parents, raised in Europe, he was brought up in a world of comfort and material security. Yet, by his own standards, he led a wild life, getting into minor trouble, driving cars at speeds of a hundred miles an hour or more. Several months before his eighteenth birthday, he agreed to help kill a young woman he had never met to keep her from testifying in court against a man he didn't even know. Eight months after the crime, he was arrested and sentenced to life imprisonment.

Roland recalls the way he felt: "Even after you get a life sentence, you don't accept it. You think you'll appeal this and that, you're not really going to do that much, maybe a few years. After a year, you say maybe a few more years. As you get more and more years in, you start accepting it more and more. It's hard as a kid, never having done time, to say I've got to do fifteen years before I see the parole board. You can't accept that. It's too much. You have to grab some kind of fantasy. Or hope that your appeal will come through. But as your appeals don't come through, you adjust to prison life. And you start saying, I can deal with it for a few more years.

"When it really started getting me was between the fourth and fifth year in prison, when you really start to realize how much time you're going to have to spend in prison. My adult life. I only had two months as an adult in the street. That's when it began to grind on me. I came to a crossroads. Am I going to get sucked into the prison mentality and deal with things physically, without talking? I was willing to hurt somebody just disrespecting you.

"In the old days, the older guys would take young kids under their wing and advise them about prison life. Get an education. Do this. Don't do that. Now there are so many ignorant guys in prison. I asked myself, 'do I want to be like them or do I want to be among the educated guys who talk about serious things?' I decided to educate myself. I had to learn to respect myself. If I don't respect my own life, how can I respect someone else's?"

"When I got fifty years, I said to the judge, 'Are you talking to me?' That's how shocked I was," said Kevin Finney, now vice-president of the Rahway chapter of the Junior Chamber of Commerce. "He said, 'Yes, I'm talking to you and if you make another outburst, I'll add more time.' So I went back to jail and I started to fall into the old ways, playing basketball and watching TV and then one day I thought I'm not going to serve all this time and not do anything for myself and one day maybe go back onto the street again, knowing only the same things I knew when I came in to prison."

Ned Woodley is one of the most physically awesome men in the prison. He is a weight lifter who has disciplined himself to press more than four hundred pounds on the bench. Yet, despite his physical strength, he was seized by despair during his early years in prison.

"When I was going to school", Ned recalls, "I was a guy who didn't want to listen to nothing. One of the reasons was because the other kids were smarter than me. So that was one of the things against me. I tried to replace that with playing all the time, messing with people, getting into trouble. I got suspended from school. I played hooky. I beat guys up. I robbed them. They kicked me out of class because I was in trouble all the time. They sent me to a special school. All boys. There were no girls. The big question was who's tougher than the next guy? That's the way it was. To impress the others, I used to drive a different stolen car to school every day. That's the only thing I wanted to do, be tougher than the next guy. Then I quit school. I just started a life of crime. I didn't have to do it. I worked. I always had a good job. Drugs was never a serious problem. I just wanted to rob.

"I was arrested for an assault in a school. I was taken and locked up for the first time. I cried. I did. I cried. I had never been locked up in a cell. But I was still thinking wrong. I was thinking what I was gonna do next . . . They sent me to reformatory. When I came out, I was really tough. You couldn't tell me nothing. I started doing house stickups. I didn't know why I was doing it. I didn't have to give nobody no money. I was still working and making money. But as soon as I finished work, I would go out and rob.

"I always said to myself one of these days I'm going to be going to prison. I knew I was going but I didn't know when. Or for how long. I felt my luck was running out and they were going to get me sooner or later. They finally got me at my

Lifers' President Harvey George in computer class where he tutors.

partner's house. I was watching a cartoon on TV and the police broke in. I thought I was going to beat it. I didn't want no deal. That would be copping out and I never copped out on anything in my life. The judge, he gave me forty-three to fifty years. I didn't believe that. I thought he was crazy. The first thing that went through my mind was 'how am I gonna do all that time?' When I got into Trenton, when I walked down this long tunnel, and the guards told me turn into this cell and I saw that tiny toilet they had and that little-bitty bed, I say to myself, 'how can I do all this time in this cell?' You ain't got nothing else. Just got this cell. You're locked in. You just sit there and wait for somebody to let you out. What hit my mind then was the first time I got locked up. When I was locked in that little cell when I was fourteen and started crying. I was crying now but I was crying on the inside. It was the wrong time to start thinking about that kind of stuff. I should have been thinking about it when I was out on the street, but I didn't. I even thought of killing myself. I thought why don't I just go ahead and end it right now, because there was no way in the world I could do all this time. My life was finished. I ain't no good. Why don't I go ahead and get me a little razor and finish it off? Why not finish it off? I really didn't care about anything anymore. Life wasn't worth anything. Right after I arrived, I saw a guy with a radio in his hand come up on a guy and beat him to death and everybody just walked by. It really shook me up. I wondered why nobody stopped this guy. Everyone just minded their own business. I did too.

"There's nobody you can talk to when you're facing all that time. You don't want to talk. What can they tell you? Nobody can tell you what to do. You gotta sit down and think to yourself, How can I get through it. Can I do it? I just imagine what I could have done with my life before I done all those wrong things. I look at these guys on TV and all that body building stuff. I could have done those things. I could have played football. I was very good at that. There were a lot of things I could have done. But I never saw any option beside robbing. I never thought I should do things like get into school, better my life. Till four or five years after I was in prison, I began to realize that I could get out one day. I learned to read better, write better. I began to think that maybe I could do something with my life after all."

Transformation begins in prison when a man first comes to grips with himself and starts to realize who he is and what he has done. If he is willing to change his attitude and life, he can draw upon a number of resources within prison to pull himself up. Some men in prison begin by taking advantage of the educational programs that are offered. Richard Kneif, the director of education at East Jersey State Prison, prides himself on his school. "I have tried to provide a normal school environment. The rooms are painted in bright colors. There are no bars on the windows. The classes are small and the men change rooms at the end of the hour as they would in a regular high school."

Every year about 150 men are enrolled in the school program. While enrollment is open and anyone can attend, many men cannot afford to go to school. In the prison hierarchy of jobs, school is considered to be semiskilled and pays between $1.75 and $2.20 a day. By comparison, a job in the kitchen pays up to $4.00 a day.

The school has three basic kinds of students, those who

are seeking to earn a high school diploma, those who are taking college courses, and those who are struggling to attain literacy. At the high school level, the school offers classes in science, English, mathematics, social studies, and computer science. The goal for men in these classes is to pass the GED (General Equivalency Diploma) and earn a high school diploma. Approximately one-third of the men who enroll in the high school program do this.

When Nelson Guzman came to prison, he was a drug addict who had killed a man during a robbery for drug money. He was spinning so hard that he spent the first four years in "ad seg." "When I came to prison, I didn't know nothing about myself, my culture. I couldn't read and I couldn't write. I had this young girlfriend. I had a lot of love for her. She wrote me, but I couldn't read her letters. It bothered me that another man had to read her letters to me and write my letters to her. I never knew if he was telling me everything or saying what I wanted him to say. I learned how to read and write in lockup. I used to take a dictionary with me into solitary and each day learn four or five new words, memorize the word and know the definition and how to spell it. Two guys educated me about my Latin culture. When I got out of solitary, I then started taking classes to get my high school degree. It took years. I flunked the test three times—three times! Until I finally passed! But I wouldn't give up. It made me feel good when I passed. It made me feel I accomplished something."

"When I came to prison, I had a sixth-grade education," Harvey George recalls. "But I had an advantage. I could read, I could always read. My aunt had made a deal with me when

I was a kid. I liked to read Superman and Archie comics, and my aunt would buy them for me, but only if I would read the classic comics. I liked reading Charles Dickens. Years later that attitude I had as a child was brought back by a teacher in prison school. She said to me that if I had the proper attitude, I could accomplish anything. People would be willing to help me. If I had a bad attitude, nobody would do anything for me. There was this one teacher who taught touch typing. I complained that I didn't need that. She put me in my place and I learned to touch type. And man, when I started dealing with law, that was the best blessing ever happened to me! I didn't know I would need to know how to type so bad! And what made me so above the other guys was that they could only hunt and peck while I was there looking at my books. She used to tell me, 'sell yourself through your attitude.' As a result, I never had a problem with the other guys because of my attitude. Guys would say 'what you got to smile about?'

"Another of my teachers told me that there are two ways to do this time, down and dirty or you can pick the ball up and carry it. You get the ball, you run—if anybody tackles you, fall forward and scramble for the goal. At that time, I thought he was talking. But even when I was getting into the negative things in jail, getting high, being slick—I was a country boy and guys here seemed to know a lot more than I did, I always went to school. Between school and Islam, I began to study for me. My study became intense. I was able to get past drugs. I began to study Islam and that taught me to learn other things. I would go to the Koran and read and then I would go to school. I got my GED. Then I took college courses. I studied law. It wasn't any great reform stuff. It was just that I was hungry to know. I had come upon a great discovery. I learned how to use the computers. I learned data base, spread sheet, how to formulate documents. I had to learn programs without the book because the book was missing. I was teaching guys who didn't know anything about computers. It was that hunger to know that made me and still makes me want to absorb everything. I was like a human vacuum cleaner."

Some men are self-taught, like "Goldie" Boone, who first educated himself, then educated others. "When I first got here, I paid guys to read books to me until my memory absorbed what they was reading. When I absorbed it, then I would look at the book and teach myself the alphabet. Now I teach college courses, I teach law, I teach remedial reading, I teach self-awareness.

"Two-thirds of the population in prison cannot read or write or comprehend reading or writing. That contributes to the high rate of recidivism. I began to hold classes to teach others to combat the ignorance in this place. When I first started the classes, they were a flop. For six months, nobody came. Then I used to pay guys to come to class. I gave them packs of cigarettes to learn to read and write. I gave them bonuses. I gave them cookies and candies and sodas. And when people heard I was doing that, people started coming. They didn't come for the purpose of education. They came for the munchies. But I wouldn't let them leave the room. I started lecturing by standing in front of the door, blocking it so they couldn't sneak out. Some of the guys dropped out. Those who were serious stayed.

"The most difficult thing was to get guys to accept the

rules. I had to expound on the rules. They hate to follow the rules. When there's a rule in English, they don't listen to it. Once they learn the rules, they're able to understand the basic components of language. It's the same problem they have in here and on the outside. Once they learn the rules in prison and in society, they will not have problems. It's difficult at times to get through but fortunately God gave me the ability to reach human hearts."

Some men educate themselves in prison through a network of other self-educated prisoners. They then pass on what they have learned to others, share books they have read, and transmit their knowledge of the world to one another. Charles Allen is one of these men. He first received his education while in solitary confinement at Trenton State Prison, before he came to East Jersey State Prison, and discovered that self-education has its risks.

"I was ignorant before I came to prison. It was in the 1970s and the world was in revolution but as far as I was concerned what was happening could have been on another planet. I had never heard of Ho Chi Minh. I had never heard of Che Guevara. I had never heard of Mao Zedong. I had never heard of the heads of African states, Patrice Lumumba. I had no idea what Malcom X's platform was. I never understood the CIA's involvement in Chile. I found out exactly how ignorant I was and I wanted to do something about it. And when you get hungry, you want to know more and more. And you get a label put on you because of what you read and who you hang out with. We were debating all sorts of things, the values of socialism, or black history, or different theories of economics. We would be debating the criminal justice system. We talked about ourselves. What was your turning point? Where did you go wrong? It was a combination of education and counseling. I was able to come to terms with my own life. They thought I was capable of spreading leftist ideas, communist ideas, throughout the prison. That's what kept me in solitary so long because of the people I met. I was considered a troublemaker. Yet they did me a favor by keeping me locked up. Before then I was thinking about freedom as something on the outside. In solitary I learned to focus on being free inside my mind. It was the best thing that happened to me in prison."

Religion plays an important part in many men's lives in prison. Some men have deep spiritual needs and either return to the religion of their childhood or find new faith inside prison. Superintendent Arvonio acknowledges that religion is one of the most powerful forces for change within a prisoner. "I have seen men completely turn around because of suddenly finding something to believe in."

"My best friend, a white officer at the county jail, introduced me to the Lord and His powers," John Stewart says. "He's become my family, my best friend, my brother, everything. Until he showed me, I never thought about the Bible before. I had never really saw one, except for the cover. I began to read and I started to wonder about a lot of things I didn't understand. That and his friendship helped me see that a lot of things didn't matter anymore—gambling, getting high. In the course of my time in prison, the Lord has blessed me many times. When I thought I couldn't handle things, He has always done something to lighten the burden of my hardship."

Pete Foster found that reading the Bible helped him out

of despair. He was particularly moved by the passage in Saint John in which the infirm wait by the pool for the angel of God to move the water so that those who immerse themselves in it can be cured.

For King Webster, the road to God came about the hard way: "One day, I had some heroin, some cocaine in my cell at Trenton and I speedballed and shot it up. I was unconscious for four days. I had overdosed. When I woke up, I felt I had died and come back to life. I suddenly felt that God had reached down and grabbed me. I took all the drugs I had and I flushed them down the toilet. I was determined to change myself. I began to study the Bible and read about religion, about men like Dietrich Bonhoeffer, the German minister who defied Hitler. I became a licensed minister. I adopted the philosophy that when I look good God looks good and that from now on my life would be a reflection of God's."

"You just get tired of being one of the walking, living dead," Yusuf Shaheed adds. "The first thing a man has to do to change when he is in a penitentiary is to address himself, his heart. He has to look at himself without fear. How did I get here? If it's my fault, I have to change. We have to find models to learn. I had to re-create a relationship with my Lord. I must not let despair cheat me of my life.

"I looked around for examples to follow. There were men I saw who I admired. They had self-control and discipline. These guys had twenty years in and the calmness in them was incredible. Their control was admirable. I wanted to incorporate in my own character the positive attributes I saw in other individuals."

For many black prisoners, Islam, which means submis-

Islam and Christianity meet the spiritual needs of many prisoners.

sion to the will of God, has become their religion. For them, Islam, with its historic ties to the Middle East and Africa, suits their spiritual and intellectual needs. While there are several Islamic groups inside East Jersey State Prison, they cooperate through an Islamic council on which they are all represented.

Rasheed Ali credits his survival in prison to his belief in God, in Allah, which, he says, "helped me to be strong. I would have fell victim to the stuff that happens in prison, to bitter feelings of remorse and sadness. But Islam doesn't let you dwell on them. It shows you that despair sickens you and disrupts your whole physical and spiritual being."

For both Bilal Abdul-Aziz, a minister of the Nation of Islam, and Dawud Abdul-Wasi, a Sunni Muslim, Islam was the transforming force in their lives. "I decided that I was going to put my life in order," Dawud Abdul-Wasi recalls. "I decided that I was going to put away the hypocritical relationship that I had with my Lord. And I was going to try to do something with myself. I came into Islam wholeheartedly. I had met a man who advised me that I should go back to school, that the important thing was to keep my body clean and pure, not in what I eat but mentally and physically. In the process, he restored self-esteem in me.

"Without Islam, we would be tyrants," Dawud Abdul-Wasi continues. "There are two major sins—two great ones above the others on which Allah is particularly hard. One is if you put other gods before him. And the second is that you take your own life. The life I was living, we were definitely on a mission. The life we lived in which we would stick people up—they were definitely crazy things, the drugs we were using, you just had to be death struck. I remember, this one kid,

I passed by his cell, sitting there with this spike in his arm. And I said to him, 'Brother, how we love death, how we love death.'

"When we came in here with the attitude we had—with the murder we had in our hearts. If it wasn't for Allah, I would probably be on death row somewhere. I probably would be running around. I'm a shepherd, not a sheep—I would probably be a shepherd with my sheep, robbing people, stealing anything that anybody had, and if I still was using drugs, the weak ones would never have no drugs. I would take it from them. And when I look at the drug dealers and others in this place, I say 'Praise to Allah.' "

Bilal Abdul-Aziz agrees. "There is no question that Allah saved my life. Prison was a blessing for me. It saved me from getting killed. I was prepared to kill somebody. I was an angry individual. I had been fighting since I can remember. As a teenager, we used to shoot each other with zip guns. We used rifles on each other. I had never shot anybody. The first time I shot somebody, I killed them. I killed one of the members of the gang. My boss talked me into doing it. I thought it was gang business. What I didn't know was that my boss was manipulating me, that he really wanted the guy dead because he was fooling around with his wife and wanted him out of the way.

"Another time I was driving in my car. I was looking for this particular guy. To shoot him, I wasn't going to kill him. Just wound him as a warning. I was driving around looking for him and I saw him on the street. I pulled over and he said to me, 'Hey, I hear you're looking for me. What do you want to do, shoot me?' I'm thinking to myself that this fool thinks I'm not going to shoot him. I pulled my gun to shoot. I didn't know he had two other guys with him. They came up behind me on the passenger side and fired. And the bullets missed! If I had stayed out in the streets, I'd probably be dead by now. So Allah in His infinite wisdom said 'let Me get this fool off the street because somewhere else I'm going to need him down the line.'

"When we first came into Islam," Abdul-Aziz continues, "we were in the mud. Islam is the detergent that agitates the dirt off of you and makes you clean. When you put laundry in the washing machine, the detergent agitates, agitates, agitates until it beats the dirt out. That's what Islam does to your soul. It beats on it till it makes it clean."

If education and religion are available to most men, psychological help is limited. It is almost a contradiction to talk of therapy in prison. Therapy is a constructive process—prison, a destructive environment.

Willie Allen expresses the emotional pain that underlies the veneer of toughness. "This place puts your feelings on hold. I ain't cried in so long. I guess the day that I do break down and cry, it's going to look like a rainstorm. You give the impression that you're a hard-nosed guy, nothing affects you, when it's really not that at all. You feel pain inside, but you keep it within. If I ever let go, I might have a nervous breakdown."

"In prison you don't reveal your emotions," Qahhar Saahir adds. "When I heard my brother had died, I didn't cry. I tried to be strong, to show that I can deal with this. I told my mother "I can't cry. I want to but it won't come out. If I do, I'm afraid I won't stop. I had a fear of crying. I just don't know how to deal with it. A week later, when I heard my grandmother died, that hit me. It hurt more than anything. Everything I was holding back came out. I had to have one of the guys help me back to my cell."

For the most part, therapy in prison is designed to help prisoners adjust to the realities of prison life—and hopefully to the outside world when they are released. Men in therapy talk about their feelings, their grievances, the conditions of their confinement, their plans to reconstruct their lives, and the reasons they committed crimes.

Tony Lorraine is one of the few men in prison who has received long-term therapeutic treatment aimed at resolving some of the deep emotional problems that have plagued him throughout his life.

Tony was raised in a middle-class, Italian family in Philadelphia. As a small child he was psychologically brutalized by his father. When he was six his mother left home, driven out by his father's behavior. His young life filled with rage and anger, Tony killed his girlfriend during a quarrel when he was seventeen. Sentenced to prison for fifteen years as a juvenile, he was released after three years. Six months later he killed an employee of a store in which he worked when she surprised him in the act of robbing the safe. He was sentenced to two life terms in prison as a multiple offender.

In 1981 Tony began one-on-one therapy in prison. He started to examine the emotional problems that lay behind his violence. At the same time, he met a woman whom he married while in prison, even though he had many years of jail time ahead of him. The marriage didn't last. When his wife divorced him, Tony attempted suicide. He almost suc-

Group counseling sessions address the emotions of life in prison.

ceeded. Declared dead at the hospital, a nurse happened to notice a flutter in his pulse and saved his life.

Today Tony is a facilitator for the Long Term Offenders Support Group, which is a group-counseling program for men serving life or long sentences. In the group session, men deal with the problems and emotions of everyday life in prison. They examine their feelings and their relationships with others both inside and on the outside. They try to gain some insight into their behavior and the reasons for getting into trouble in the first place. "Rehabilitation fails," Tony observes, "because people do not understand why they did what they did. They admit to what they did, but rarely find the reason why. A person has to be motivated to find the answers. If you force therapy on him, you can't expect too much."

Dr. Kay Herud, chief psychologist at East Jersey State Prison, notes: "Some men sincerely want to understand themselves and change their behavior. Therapy can really help them if their problems aren't too deep and if they are motivated to change. But while it can help individual prisoners, therapy is just not available on a large scale to most men in prison. And prison itself isn't a therapeutic environment to begin with. So we are constantly swimming against the tide to save a relatively small number of individuals. And sometimes we win."

Far from home, but still not forgotten.

FAMILIES

CHAPTER 11

It is one of the sad facts of East Jersey State Prison that out of the 2,200 men imprisoned there, only an estimated 15 percent receive visits. Many serving long-term sentences have been forgotten by friends and families. The longer the sentence, the more likely it is that a man may become estranged from loving relationships in the outside world.

Unfortunately, many men in prison see their parents' efforts to steer them in the right direction only after they are in jail. Kevin Finney recalls, "My parents tried to raise me right. They tried to discipline me. But I wouldn't listen. I tell my mother now that after all our talks, I never really listened to you. And now I can see that you never told me wrong and I love you for that. I know the hurt that I caused her. When my mother was on the street, she was so beautiful and so young. And now, when I see her and age is coming on, I see the hurt inside her and it's my fault. And the pain in her face. To make up for the hurt I caused my mother, I changed my whole attitude and everything. All I want to do is get back on the street and be successful."

Willie Allen notes that men inside always keep up a front for their families. "We try to prove to our families we can make it. We know that they're hurting for us, we know that they fear for us, but we harden ourselves, we smile even though we're hurting inside. We try to show that we're dealing with it. We know how hard it is for them when people ask about us, they have to say we are in jail. We know that it's not only us that serves time, that they serve time with us."

Relationships with those on the outside are always fragile and the reality is that a man serving a life sentence is more a beggar than a chooser. As Roland Gebert has observed, "If a girl wants to come see you, she'll come see you. You can't put demands on her. Parents drift away, too. Mothers die. Fathers die. Brothers and sisters lose interest. It's part of the price you pay. And in some ways, it's easier. All you have to deal with is prison."

It is unusual for marriages to last when a man has been sentenced to life in prison. Under today's law, a lifer must serve at least twenty-five years without guarantee of parole when his minimum time is up. Many lifers divorce or break off their relationships with their wives or girlfriends when they first come to prison. Over the years, however, some hope to meet a woman while they are in prison, usually through the wife or girlfriend of another man. Their dream, or perhaps illusion, is that they will find a love on the outside that will help sustain them through their sentence. Those who are more practical-minded seek a woman to visit and bring them food packages. Others use women to buy them things, smuggle drugs, and run errands for them on the outside. Imo Allen has a more down-to-earth approach: "How can I marry a woman who I see only a few hours a week? I don't know anything about her, what kind of a person she is, how she keeps her house, makes a budget, raises her children. I also wonder why a woman would be willing to spend fifteen years with me when I'm in jail. I don't think I want to be with a woman who would do that. She must be crazy."

Raab Ali Kahn disagrees. President of the Rahway Forum, a group that helps prisoners and their families, he and his wife, Sharonda, have been married for eleven years. "To keep a marriage going that long when your husband is in prison, you need a sense of humor and you have to take one step at a time," Sharonda maintains. "And it takes an awful lot of creative thinking. For example, I try to include my husband in everything I do. When I do my hair in a certain way, I tell people 'he likes it when I do my hair like that.' On New Year's Eve, I have a party for him. I dress up, set the table, light the candles, put out the plates, and offer a toast to him. Sometimes, I feel like I'm living in a fairy tale. And sometimes, I'm miserable. But I'm committed to him. I remember him when he was on the streets. He was like a runaway balloon—you know when you blow it up and then let it go and all the air runs out and it flies all over the place. But he has changed since he's been in prison."

Raab Ali Kahn credits his wife for being responsible for much of that change. "She's been my teacher in religion and with my relationships with my children. I fell in love with her when I first heard her voice on the telephone and it's lasted through all these years. And my faith in Islam serves as the cement for me to help bind our relationship."

For Dawud Abdul-Wasi, his faith helped him over the

rough spots in his marriage. "There was a lot of times my wife couldn't deal with where I was and the circumstances of being confined. And I could not fulfill manhood and she could not fulfill womanhood. We did not find those great moments of peace that we would like to have found, but in placing our love of each other in the forefront and in placing our fear of Allah in the forefront, they have been great motivating factors.

"It gets depressing at times. It's a very lonely life. But the mere fact that we can communicate by phone and write letters helps. It is depressing not to be able to express your love the way you want. You have to make concessions."

Fathers and sons in good-natured play . . .

and heart-to-heart discussion.

Communication is an essential part of such a relationship. "I never had such a close relationship before," Helen Melvins says of her husband, Max. "He's become so understanding in the years I've known him. We talk about everything and we're on the telephone every day. If I'm going somewhere, to a restaurant or a business meeting, I leave my number in case Max wants to reach me. I want him to be able to talk to me whenever he wants."

Helen knew Max in his wild days on the street. When he was imprisoned, she began to write to him as a friend. The friendship grew into a romance. In the beginning, she would drive over four hundred miles to visit him each weekend. Finally she moved near Rahway to be close to him.

"Most of my family and friends who know about Max are supportive of our relationship," Helen says. "But some people don't understand why you get involved with a man who's in prison. Well, I don't think they can ever understand unless it happens to them."

Max recalls the difficulty they had in getting married. According to prison regulations, no prisoner can be married without the institution's permission. Max and Helen were first given permission; then it was denied. "The prison said that it wasn't in the best interest of myself, Helen, and the community for me to get married. So I said, 'Okay, let's see.' I got a lawyer who knew the system. He sent a letter to the superintendent at that time, saying that if the prison was going to deny me permission to marry, he was going to sue them. Two weeks later, I got permission."

Although East Jersey State Prison allows contact visits three days a week, it is difficult for a woman to visit prison. She must arrive early and may be given a thorough physical examination before being allowed in. The search proved so humiliating to Edward Barry's mother the first time she visited him in Trenton State Prison that she never came to see him again. "For six years, until she died, I didn't see my mother again," Barry bitterly recalls, "because she felt so embarrassed at the way she was examined."

During the winter, visits are held inside a large room; during the summer, they take place outside in a large open area. While contact is allowed between the prisoners and their wives and girlfriends, many find it degrading to have to

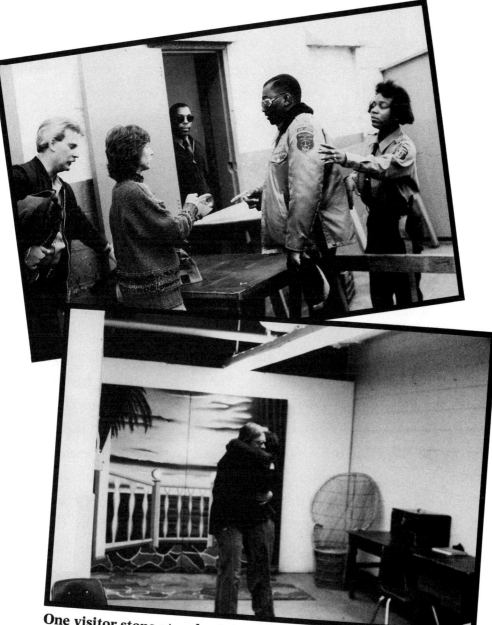

One visitor stops at a checkpoint for inspection, before greeting her fiancé.

show affection in public, under the watchful eyes of officers. Director of Operations Steve Maggi would like to see conjugal visits allowed. "I would set aside a certain area where guys could spend a weekend with their families once a month, as some prisons do have in other states. I think it's important in order to keep the family together. Husband and wife could have normal sexual relations rather than grope at each other in the visiting area. It's better all the way around."

Occasionally visitors are subjected to other inconveniences. Lydia George, Harvey George's wife, recalls the day that all the visitors had to wait inside the prison for hours while the police searched for a person who was trying to escape. "When they discovered that a prisoner was missing, they wouldn't let any of us go. We had to stand there while they searched. What he had done was to put on a wig his wife had brought him and put on a false beard. He looked really odd. He was standing behind two women who were furious about having to wait. One of them said, 'If I find him, they won't have to worry about bringing him back. I'll kill him myself.' And when he was discovered, trying to sneak out with the visitors, the women began to throw things at him, they were so angry at him for making them wait all that extra time."

Why are women willing to marry or make long-term commitments to men serving life terms? What motivates them to undergo long separations, and to forego sexual relationships, children, and a normal family life? Tariq Commander sees advantages for a woman in such a relationship. "There's not any woman who gets more attention than a woman involved with a man in prison. He writes all the time, he calls her, he asks about her, he worries about her, he buys her things, he helps her out with money when he can. She needs a television set, he may work his butt off for four months to buy one for her and the kids. She's treated like a queen."

Dr. Herud points out that the motivations of women who become involved with prisoners vary. "Some are attracted to violence. On the other hand, the women have a guy they can do a lot for. He's there for them and they're not threatened by other women. Their self-esteem raises. They feel very needed and appreciated. Some women feel they are saviors and can help them or redeem a prisoner. They really get a lot of satisfaction for that.

"But a relationship with a prisoner is not a normal life," Dr. Herud continues. "It's not a real life; it's a partial life. Yet some men and women make it work and the relationship continues after the man is released. It takes exceptional people to do this."

For many lifers who came to prison in their teens, there is a good chance that they will be young enough when released to establish a family life on the outside. This possibility is one reason why many women say they are willing to wait. But there are a few lifers whose future is uncertain and who, because of either the severity of their crimes or the public reaction to them, may spend many more years in jail.

Bob Conklin has been in prison for twenty-one years, three-and-a-half of which he spent on death row for a double homicide committed during a robbery. He has never forgotten the last words his trial judge said to him: "May God have mercy on your soul." In 1971 the United States Supreme

Court overturned New Jersey's death penalty and Bob was given a life sentence plus twenty years. Six years ago, when he was eligible for parole for the first time, he received a twelve-year hit (sentence), one of the longest ever given to a prisoner at East Jersey State Prison.

The length of his sentence was no deterrent for his wife, Marge, who first met Bob through a friend whose husband was also in prison. She began to write to him and then came down for a visit. "I knew I was going to be involved with Bob the moment I laid eyes on him." They were married several years later.

Marge is always one of the first to arrive at the prison every visiting day. "On family day, when I can spend a whole day with Bob rather than just a half-day, I get to the prison at 3 A.M. sometimes and wait six hours so I can be among the first to enter. Once I almost got arrested because the police saw me parked and wanted to know what I was doing. They thought I might be planning an escape."

Why do I do it? My love for Bob. I've never known a love anything on the street like we have. He is so considerate, so thoughtful. We talk about everything. We communicate. He has such love for me and my family. When they need anything he helps out."

Bob's relationship with his wife's family was not smooth at first. "My wife's family did not accept me at first," he remembers. "I was glad I had told her all the details about my crime because they went to the library and looked it up in old newspapers and showed it to her. She said, 'yes, I know all about it.' Then when they saw the way I treated my wife, they saw past one two-minute episode in my life and accepted me."

Marge says that her children have no problem accepting Bob as their father. "Neither one has tried to hide me or are ashamed." His eleven-year-old stepson, Jimmy, says, "I tell my friends my dad's in prison. Sometimes the kids call me the 'son of a jailbird.' That hurts." "Why do you tell them then?" Bob asks. "Because I'm not ashamed of you," Jimmy replies.

The hardest thing for some men is to confess their crimes to someone they love. For Tony Lorraine, whose victims were women, it was even more painful.

Tony met his present fiancé, Sandy, as a result of the television documentary *Scared Straight*. "I was living in California and my son was getting into trouble," Sandy recalls, "playing hooky, stealing, being arrested. I couldn't communicate with him and nobody else seemed to be able to, either. One night I came home, feeling very low about what was happening to him. I turned on the television and there was the film *Scared Straight*. It sounds like a movie script but that's exactly what happened. I watched the program and thought 'maybe they can help my son.' He was then in detention in a youth home. The next day I called him and asked if he and the others had watched the program. He said that he had. 'I got the message, Mom.' He really seemed to mean it. I wrote to the Lifers' Group, thanking them for what they did. Tony answered my letter."

A correspondence began, followed by phone calls. Sandy was extremely hesitant at first. "I expected to correspond with someone who may have had a fourth-grade education. I was surprised to find that Tony was an intelligent, articulate man, who showed a great deal of concern and care for me and my son. In fact, no man ever showed more concern for my son than Tony did."

Tony began to talk with Sandy's son to help him straighten out his life. The relationship between Sandy and Tony began to develop into a romance. "I tried to counter what was happening by thinking how absurb this whole thing was. Tony was in prison. I didn't know how long he would be there or if I was willing to commit myself to stay with him and help him rebuild his life. And I really didn't know what his crimes were. He had written to me about them, but I knew he was holding back about them and avoiding dealing with

A visit with Mom and Dad.

them." Sandy traveled to New Jersey and met Tony. It was a moment of truth. Sandy wanted to know what Tony had done.

"When I first told Sandy that I had committed two homicides," Tony states, "I didn't go into any great detail about them. I didn't want to scare her off and, quite frankly, I didn't know how serious the relationship would be. But as it became more serious, then I had to face up to the fact. She kept pressing me, and the more she pressed the more reluctant I became to talk. She accused me of not being open with her. I said, 'I am open with you. I tell you everything that's going on here.' Then she replied, 'That's not what I mean. You're not open emotionally.' My answer was 'I'm not, because after eighteen years in prison, to be vulnerable is to be hurt.' Finally I realized that if I was going to have a serious relationship with her, I had to tell her everything. So I gave her the transcript of my trial and said, 'read this.' I expected never to hear from her again. When I next saw her, she said, 'I knew it was like this. I just wanted to hear it from you.'"

Sandy moved to New Jersey to be near Tony. Friends wondered why she would choose to get involved with a man who had killed two women and who might spend many more years in prison, despite his extraordinary efforts to deal with his problems and prepare himself for return to the outside world.

"It's funny," Sandy says, "I have never felt physically in danger from Tony. I was afraid of being hurt emotionally because I discovered that some men in prison have a number of "fiancés" who visit them, each of which is not aware of the others. And my son had some problems with Tony's crimes when I told him what Tony had done. But I am a Christian and I believe people deserve a chance and I have faith in Tony. He is an inner man; he has great substance, sensitivity, and understanding inside of him. We have a very deep relationship on that level and that is why I am willing to wait for him as long as it takes. He is worth waiting for. He has an awful past to overcome and I believe I can help him overcome it. I, too, have to overcome my past, which is not as difficult as his, but is difficult all the same. I feel that we can do it together."

Perhaps the hardest thing to deal with is the effect imprisonment may have on a man's children. There is a deep concern by many lifers that their children may be negatively affected. At East Jersey State Prison, this is partially offset by the fact that the visiting area is in an open space that minimizes the prison atmosphere. Contact visits are allowed and the prisoners wear ordinary street clothes. There is also a play area for younger children. Dawud Abdul-Wasi emphasizes that he and other men spend a great deal of "quality" time with their children. "I talk with them, play with them, find out how they are and what they're doing. I just don't ignore them when they're here."

One concern of the lifers is telling their children why they are in prison. Most lifers do so when they feel the children are ready. Rasheed Ali told his daughter directly, while others let their children read the transcripts of their trial. Often a lifer's parents help the children accept their father's being in jail. "They talk to them about us, encourage them to believe that it is not shameful that we are in prison," Imo Allen explains. "One of my daughters even brought her friends to meet me. My other daughter, however, didn't want her friends to know. Our job is to make them understand that we

Dawud Abdul-Wasi and his daughter—when should the children know why we are here?

are responsible for our actions, but that at the same time prison reflects the racism that exists in American society."

"No matter how much we spoil our children and tell them we love them, we feel guilty we are here and not with them," Tony Hayes concludes. When it comes time to leave, we can see the hurt on their faces and they can see the hurt on ours. They sometimes cry and some of us cry, too. They are often angry when they leave, although we don't see that anger. Their mother does though. They have to deal with it. We just go back to our cells and sit and wait for the next visit."

How realistic is it for men serving life terms in prison to

Capturing some reminders of home . . .

sustain a long-term relationship with a woman and maintain a family? "It depends strictly on the people and how mature they are," Dr. Herud observes. "One good thing about these relationships if they are relatively healthy—and that's a big 'if'—is that they can carry over to other relationships. I have seen men in prison give up negative values and acquire the positive values of the person they love. I have seen men change over a period of time because of how they got treated in a relationship. They respond when they are treated as human beings, receiving certain basic human things that you don't get in prison. A lot of these men have never really known the kind of love that some women can offer them. And it helps them change—at least in prison. The real test is, of course, what happens after they get out. And some do make it work."

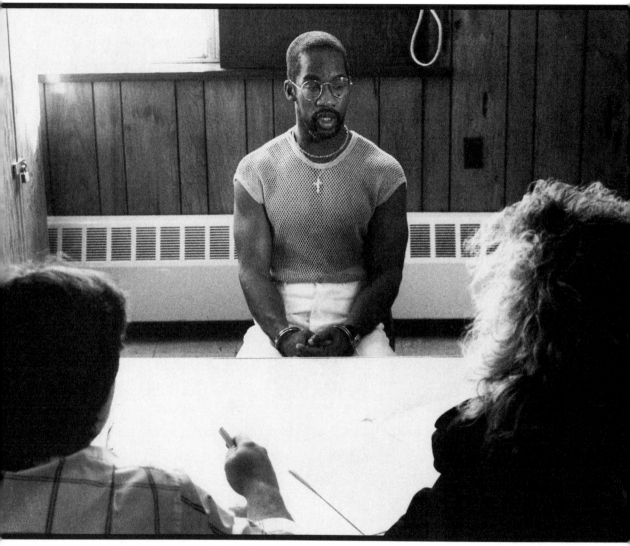

Every lifer dreams of this day.

FREEDOM

CHAPTER 12

John Chaney, wrists in handcuffs, legs bound in irons, is escorted by an officer into the room where members of the parole board wait. Like every prisoner brought before the board, John Chaney is bound as a precautionary measure to avoid any possible physical confrontation or attempt at escape—despite the effect this may have on the board.

For fifteen years John Chaney has been living for this moment—the possibility of learning, no matter how remote, that he may soon be free. Every lifer dreams of the day when he will leave prison while he still has time to enjoy life, even if such hope defies reason. Often the slimmer the chance a man may have for release, the greater is his hope, the wilder his dreams of freedom.

But while John Chaney, a deeply religious man, may pray for his release from what he calls "this tormented hell-hole, filled with fools and madmen," he knows the odds are overwhelmingly against him. He is aware that being eligible for parole and being granted parole are two different things. No man serving a life term is guaranteed a parole. Only a parole board, a pardon from the governor, or a reversal of the sentence by the courts can release him from prison. He cannot "max out" as other prisoners can, because his sentence is not for a specified number of years, but for natural life. The parole board can continue to deny him parole until the day he dies. And there are men inside prison who have committed such violent crimes that no one expects they will ever be released.

Moreover, parole boards in New Jersey seldom release lifers the first time they are eligible for parole, no matter how spotless their record inside prison, no matter how much they have changed. Often the reason is political. It is safer to keep a man in jail than to release him. No one can accuse the parole board or the politicians of being soft on crime when they keep prisoners locked up as long as possible. Yet, ironically, men who have committed homicides are the least likely group of prisoners to commit another crime once released. The return rate for them is 6.6 percent as compared to approximately 50 percent for the rest of the prison population. Superintendent Arvonio points out that after most lifers spend a certain time—far shorter than the present sentences—"the extra time becomes purely punitive. In reality, homicides are committed by people killing someone they know, a crime of passion, a one-time deal. A man can do five years and never commit another crime. You can release him after a certain period of time and you can predict what they do. He's not likely to return. But the habitual criminal—the armed robber, the dope dealer, the guy who commits aggravated assault—that's the guy that fills the jail up." And Chief Maggi and Officer James Palagonia both feel that the system should be more like that of Europe's—"much shorter sentences, but much harder time."

Once a man is eligible for parole, a hearing officer will investigate his record in prison and make a recommendation to a two-member panel of the parole board as to what they should do. While much is made of what a prisoner does in prison, no one knows how influential a good record is. In the years he has been in prison, Chaney has completed college programs, vocational training, is deeply involved in his church, and has promises of a job outside. He has no idea what effect this will have on the parole board. Sometimes the more a man accomplishes in prison, the more suspicious a parole board may be of him. They may regard this as a sign of insincerity. Yet, if he should fail to take advantage of the programs offered, it can also be regarded as a lack of proper motivation. From the lifer's point of view, it is often a no-win situation.

Once the two-member panel of the parole board has reviewed the hearing-officer's report, they will meet with John and then make their recommendation. If they recommend parole, John will appear before the full nine-member parole board, which will make the final decision as to whether or not he is to be released. If the two-member panel decides to make him serve additional time, they have two options. They can "hit" him within or outside the guidelines. A hit within the guidelines means that John will be sentenced to serve up to thirty-six additional months before he can reapply for parole. Whatever good time and work time he has earned can be used to reduce the waiting period. Those men who receive a hit outside the guidelines will be summoned before a three-member panel of the parole board, which will decide how much more time the prisoner must serve before he will again be eligible for parole. A hit outside the guidelines usually ranges from four to ten years, with about half that time canceled because of good time.

By law the parole board must consider two things in deciding whether or not to grant parole. The first is whether the board feels that the prisoner has served enough time to have been sufficiently punished for his crime. The second is the key consideration: What are the chances that a prisoner will again commit a crime if he is released? The board looks at his record to see what he has accomplished in prison. Has he learned a trade, adjusted to prison life, received therapy,

Tony Lorraine as a paralegal advises Charles Matthews.

joined constructive programs, such as the Lifers' Group? Yet, even if one has done all these things, he may still be turned down. As one former parole officer stated: "Parole boards tend to regard with suspicion a man who has had no problems inside as well as a man who has had many. People who tend to adjust well to prison life may be unable to adjust on the outside."

The parole board also bases its judgment on the degree of insight a prisoner shows into why he committed his crime, the extent of genuine remorse he feels for it, and the empathy he has for his victims. For John Chaney, these considerations are stumbling blocks. He insists he is innocent of the murder for which he was convicted. He knows that if he maintains this claim of innocence, the board will probably deny his request for parole. He has prepared himself for this, and his major concern is how long his hit will be.

The hearing begins with the two members of the parole board asking John to describe the crime he committed. Chaney hesitates for a moment before responding:

"I really can't say because I wasn't there. I only know what was told to me."

One board member shows he is not pleased with this answer. He asks Chaney to describe the crime as it was told to him. Chaney tells how he heard that a man involved in cheating others was shot to death in revenge as he sat in his car.

"Why was it necessary to shoot the man eight times?" the other board member asks.

"You ask me as if I was the one who shot him. I don't know the answer to that question."

"Well, that's what it says in the record, and all we can

go on is what we have here. After all, you were found guilty."

"I understand that, but you can see that I was convicted on the testimony of only one person and that person was lying."

"We find it hard to believe."

"Why do you find it hard to believe? It happens all the time, all the time!"

"We have to go by the records. How much more time do you think you should serve?"

"If you mean how much time should the man who did the crime serve, he should serve until he is eligible for parole—14.8 years. Any additional time is punitive. For me, one minute is too much because I didn't do it. I'm not saying I was an angel on the streets. I was dealing and using drugs. And if I was being punished for that, that would be all right and I can accept that. However, it is not logical for me to spend fifteen years here and continue to maintain my innocence, when I know that by doing so, I may be given more time than I would get if I lied and said I'm guilty. But my conscience won't let me do that. I'm in God's hands. I submitted myself to God years ago and the worst that can happen is that I will have to spend more time in here, maybe the rest of my life in here. Well, I can accept that if I have to."

After the hearing, the panel recommended a hit outside the guidelines. The decision did not come as a surprise. Chaney was aware that by maintaining his innocence he could wind up with a ten-year hit. Instead the panel gave him six years, which meant that he would be eligible to come up before the parole board in approximately three years because of good time. "It could have been worse," he said.

"What happens to us in here is that we shut down our emotions, close them off," Bob Conklin states. "This is not what the parole board is looking for. They want you to go over details of crime—relive it. Explain the circumstances. Explain why it happened. That's the most painful part. If you give flat answers because you don't want your emotions to overflow, I have to convince them that it's me that's talking and not another person. Their job is a thankless one. They're damned if they do and damned if they don't. No matter what they do, some segment of society will criticize them. Yet very few lifers repeat their crime and return to prison. Why do we have to serve such a long time? I've been locked up for twenty-one years. I'm being punished for the rising crime rate outside and I've been in here."

Occasionally, a prisoner, worn down by prison life, unable to deal with the length of his sentence and driven by a longing for freedom so powerful it consumes his every waking moment, dreams of escape. While every man in prison probably has such yearnings, for the overwhelming majority, it is only a fantasy. The barriers and the chances of being caught are so great and the consequences of being caught so punishing that few men dare to try.

José Perez was only in prison a short while before he began to dream of escape. Bitter because he felt he was wrongly imprisoned for refusing to cooperate with the police for a crime someone he knew had committed, he became obsessed with escaping shortly after he was incarcerated. "I was walking around the yard, thinking to myself, 'man what a bunch of crazy people here.' Then I looked up and saw the walls and I thought, 'hey, they ain't so big.' So I did just like I seen in the movies. I took some sheets, tied them together and then I soaked them, to keep them real wet so that they wouldn't rip. One night I went to a show in the auditorium, and I left early. The guard asked me where I was going and I said, 'the show was no good, I was going back to the wing.' As soon as I was clear, I got out through a window, got to the wall, and I attached something to the end so I could hook the sheet to the top of the wall. I threw it up about four times before it caught. Then I pulled myself up and got to the top. My belly was lying on the top and I was all set to jump down. I just wanted to make sure that the patrol car that circled the walls regularly wasn't on the other side. Just as I looked down, the wall broke under me. A big chunk of it broke off and there was this metal rod underneath that almost went through my throat. Luckily I fell back, but I also fell off the wall and back into the yard. It was almost thirty feet. I thought I killed myself. I must have laid there for fifteen minutes. Nobody heard me or saw me. Since I wasn't dead, I figured I might as well get up and try again. I broke into the shop, got another hook, tied it to the end of the sheet and again hooked the sheet to the top of the wall and began to pull myself up. Suddenly the escape alarm went off and the guard in the tower turned his big spotlight on and finally found me climbing up. I jumped down and began to run around for quite awhile, when I asked myself 'what was I running for? I wasn't going anywhere.' So I let them catch me. A lieutenant, sergeant, and three guards took me to the interrogation room. They beat me up real good. They wanted to know who helped me. I said 'no one,' even though there were guys that helped me out. They said, 'you're gonna tell us.' I said, 'I'm not gonna tell you nothing. You can beat me all day.' Finally one of the officers said, 'you better leave him alone.' He saw I was beat up real bad, so they took me to the hospital. I wanted to tell one of the nurses what happened, but the police said that I was injured 'cause I fell off the wall. I spent a year in solitary before I was released."

If escape is an improbable dream of freedom seldom pursued by men in prison, there is another dream that many men do pursue—the hope that the courts will overturn their decision. Arthur Tillman, a prisoner and a paralegal notes "that many men are here because they were ignorant of the law at the time of their trial. They did not have good representation. They may not have been innocent of a crime, but they were often improperly tried or sentenced and ended up spending many more years in prison than they would have had they had adequate counsel."

For the courts to review and overturn a decision or modify a sentence is a long process, often taking years with little chance for success. A man who appeals his sentence often has to file many legal briefs, sometimes filling out hundreds of arguments in his behalf. The process can take years. Since most men cannot afford to pay an outside lawyer to take their case, most men in prison either do the legal work themselves or rely upon the help of prison paralegals, often referred to as "jailhouse lawyers." These men are very familiar with criminal law and the appeals process.

Tony Lorraine, who had been given two consecutive life sentences after his second homicide, won a certain degree of fame within prison when he appealed his sentence and won a major victory. Tony had studied law while in prison and became an expert paralegal. He eventually earned a law degree through a correspondence course. "My argument was that the judge had overstepped his bounds by giving me two consecutive life sentences for a single crime. I had already been found guilty, was sentenced, served time and was paroled for my first crime. The judge just wanted to be sure that I was not going to get out of prison ever again if he could help it—or at least not until I was very old."

The appeals court reviewed Tony's case, congratulated him on the excellent presentation of his argument, and reduced the sentence to one life term.

Occasionally a conviction is overturned or at least a new trial is ordered by an appellate court. Such was the case of Jimmy Landano, past president of the Lifers' Group, who served fifteen years in prison for a crime he insists he didn't commit.

In August 1975, on Staten Island, New York, Landano was driving toward his mother's house when he passed what he thought was a funeral procession. "There was this line of cars on the street," he recalls "and I thought they were going to a funeral. It almost turned out to be mine. All of a sudden, I saw this car racing behind me with a guy leaning out the window with a shotgun in his hand. He was pointing it my way. My first thought was who did I insult that they'd want to kill me?" In the next moment two cars rammed Jimmy's car from each side and a policeman jumped on the hood with a shotgun in his hand and smashed it through the windshield, pointing it at Jimmy's chest. Another police officer held a gun at his neck. Thirty-five police officers surrounded the car, guns drawn. "Needless to say, I was under arrest," Jimmy notes.

Jimmy was charged with murdering a police officer

Arthur Tillman researches a case in the law library.

during a robbery of a check-cashing place. The officer had been moonlighting as an armed guard, transporting money to and from the business. Three men had been involved in the robbery and one of them had deliberately gunned down the officer in his car. Jimmy was named as the gunman by one of the robbers, a man he says he never met. "This guy knew of me through one of the other robbers, the man I believe killed the detective."

Another witness also linked Jimmy to the crime, although he was not certain about his identity. When asked by the prosecutor to pick the killer out in the courtroom, the witness pointed to Jimmy with some uncertainty and said, "That's him, ain't it?" Adding to Jimmy's difficulty was the fact that he had prior convictions involving heroin and had served time in prison, although he told the court that he had been clean for two years at the time he was arrested.

After five days of deliberations, the jury seemed hung until the judge strongly pressured them to make a decision. They finally returned a verdict. Guilty. The judge sentenced Jimmy to life in prison plus fifteen years.

"It pulled the rug from under my feet. There's no greater feeling of powerlessness when you're innocent and found guilty. I was very bitter. I was ready to eat people alive." Two things saved him from doing something destructive: the Lifers' Group and meeting his future wife, Camille.

"Working with the kids helped steady me. I was able to use my case as an example of how a past life of crime can come back to haunt you, even when you're innocent. Meeting and then marrying Camille was the most important thing. She was one of the few people I met who believed me when I said I was innocent. In prison the last thing you talk about is innocence because nobody wants to hear that."

Although she believed Jimmy to be innocent, Camille had decided to put a two-year limit on helping him get free. "If he hadn't succeeded by then, I said to myself, I was going to end the relationship. Little did I know what was in store for me. When we started to uncover evidence to show that someone else was the killer, I was certain the courts would set Jimmy free. This is America, I thought. Justice will triumph. Boy, did I have a lot to learn."

There were two grounds for a new trial. One was that the witness had been pressured, if not coerced, by the police to identify Jimmy as the killer. And the second was that the prosecution had suppressed evidence that showed that someone other than Jimmy could have been the killer.

The key witness who testified against Jimmy admitted in court that he had been pressured to do so. The trial judge refused to order a new trial. Jimmy appealed to the federal courts, which rejected his appeal, even though the district court was sympathetic to the case.

"If I had gotten the death penalty rather than a life sentence I would have been executed then, as all my appeals had been exhausted. Almost fourteen years had gone by and I had worked on my case day and night. The only hope was that some evidence would turn up that showed the prosecution had suppressed information that showed there was a possibility that someone else had committed the crime. It turned out they did."

A number of people began to help Jimmy with his case, including Neil Mullin, a well-known civil-rights lawyer, and

Jim McClosky, a minister who works to help free innocent men from jail. A document was finally found that did show the police had another suspect—one whom witnesses described as being 5 feet 8 inches tall, curly-haired and clean-shaven. None of these characteristics fit Jimmy. In 1990 the federal district court allowed Jimmy to go free on bail. Shortly afterward, the Appeals Court ruled that the case should have gone back to the trial court before it reached the federal courts. Jimmy is presently fighting this decision and against the possibility of having his bail revoked and being returned to jail.

Every lifer askes the question "What must I do to pay my debt to society in order to be free? Yusuf Shaheed, president of the Penal Reform Committee at East Jersey State Prison, says, "Society asks, 'what's going to happen to these guys once they get out of there?' There are guys in here who don't have no problem spending five, ten, fifteen years in prison and getting out and doing the same thing. Because nobody's helping them. Society is crying about the plague of crime. The crime plague. Yet nobody wants to take a step toward changing human life, making an attempt to change the conduct of men inside jail. If we say we want our children to grow up safe and intelligent, we provide schools for them, we make sure they have proper housing. If we say we want a better society from men coming out of prison, then we have to help change the minds of men. We can't change it for them. They have to want to do that themselves. We have to create atmospheres. We have to create opportunities conducive for that kind of change.

"There are certain things in prison that exist that are

geared to keep a man down, that keep his morality down, keep his self-perception down . . . and they know this. You got to build that man back up. He needs encouragement, all the support he can get. We understand that they are afraid of us out there and we understand why they're afraid. And we're afraid of what it's like outside after so many years. We rely on the system to give us the right answers, the same way you relied on the courts to convict us. You should rely on the system to set us free—don't convict us all over again. If our record reflects a pattern of stability, a pattern of responsibility, a pattern of maturity, what more can you expect? The parole board says, 'well we don't know if you'll commit a crime again or not.' My answer is 'yes, you don't know. Maybe it's not for you to know. Maybe it's something for time to tell.' "

The dream of freedom persists. "Last night," says Tony Lorraine, "I was watching TV and they had this scene on the beach. Now I hate the beach, I hate the ocean, and I hate the sand. But what I wouldn't give to experience that."

Two months after his dream, Tony met with the parole board. He was hoping they would give him a six-year hit and feared that he would receive as many as twelve years. At his hearing some members of the panel wanted to give him an additional twelve to fifteen years because he had committed a second killing after he had been paroled almost twenty years ago. But everyone on the panel was impressed by the efforts he had made to change himself. Their final decision was ten years. This means that Tony will have to serve six more years before he will be eligible for parole—and go through the process once again.

What are the chances of a lifer making it on the outside

once he is released? Statistically, they are pretty good. Relatively few lifers return to prison after they are paroled. Some men have matured enough not to return to crime. Some have gained enough insight into themselves to be able to control their impulses and build up a tolerance for frustration. But after being locked away for fifteen years or more, it is hard for a man to return to society and try to start a new life for himself. Prison sometimes becomes a second home to him, a place where he gets respect from his peers. "It makes us feel good to be a big fish in a small pond than a small fish in a big one," Willie Allen observes. He speaks from bitter experience. Two years after he was released on parole, he returned to prison. He recalls the experience:

"I fooled myself into believing that I had changed enough and that society hadn't changed and that I was strong enough to deal with my problems by myself. I thought it was a sign of weakness that I needed help. But right from the beginning, I was torn in two. Part of me wanted the new life—family, job, respectability—and part of me wanted the old life on the streets. The streets still had a powerful attraction for me. I used to drive to my old neighborhood and sit in a parked car and watch the people on the streets. I made the excuse that I was going to visit my family, who still lived there. But what was pulling me back was drugs. I thought I could hang out with my sister and her friends who were doing drugs without my doing them. They warned me to keep away from them. I wouldn't listen. Every time I had a problem, I thought of getting high and escaping from it. Then, when my girlfriend lost our child that she was carrying, I blew it. I started taking drugs again after two years without them. I lost my job and I returned to the old life. I remember sitting in a room all day with a gun. I had freaked out so much that I carried on this conversation with the gun. I had no money and I needed money and I imagined the gun was saying to me, 'pick me up and go out and get money.' And I kept saying, 'No, I won't do that.' But eventually the gun won and I went back into the streets. Everybody could see what was happening to me. I was speeding, but I couldn't see it. They told me to slow down. I didn't listen and wound up back in jail.

"I hadn't learned my lesson then. But as soon as they locked me up again, they could have let me loose, because I then knew what I didn't know before. You need support on the outside to make it. You need all the support you can get. You need family, wives, parents, girlfriends, counselors. All the lifers who left here and made it—George Merritt, Malcolm Scott, James Artis, Jimmy Landano—they all had people out there helping them. And they used that help. I didn't. That was my problem. I should have gone to my parole officer, who was a pretty good guy, and told him that I wasn't making it and needed help. Now I can say that. Now I'll ask to be discharged right into a drug program when I see the parole board again. And that's what makes the difference. Nobody who leaves prison and has a drug problem—and that's most of us—is going to make it without help."

Portrait of a lifer: the oldest man in East Jersey State Prison.

CONCLUSION

Lieutenant August tells the following story. "I got a call from this kid's father and he tells me that a couple of years ago his kid was getting into trouble with drugs and such and he came to the program and it straightened him out. So the kid wanted to do something for the Lifers' Group and his father said that his kid was now studying music and could he come out to the prison and give a concert?"

"So I arranged the concert and I forgot that on the night of the concert there were also boxing matches and it was hard rounding up the guys. Anyhow, I finally get everybody together and I put them in the chapel and I locked the door so nobody could slip out. In comes this kid with his father carrying a musical instrument. And he's dressed in a tuxedo. They put this instrument in the front of the room and the kid first thanks the Lifers' Group for what they did for him and then he begins to play—Mozart, Chopin, stuff like that. Now most of these guys—and I include myself—have never heard an instrument like this before. None of them listen to that stuff. In prison? I was sure they were all dying to go to the boxing matches, but no, they sat very quiet and listened and they applauded at the end of each piece. It was like a concert, you know at the opera. They really liked it. You know what the instrument was? A freaking harp! A gold-plated harp! And here we are, a cop and a bunch of cons serving life terms for homicides sitting in the chapel listening and enjoying fancy music on this harp. And it was because of the program that the kid was playing it."

Many teenagers are doing things today they might not have done were it not for the Juvenile Awareness Program. Some are in college; others have their own careers and businesses. They have married and are raising families, teaching others what they once learned in a prison. But as one prisoner notes, "what goes round comes round," and those who have visited the program have left their mark on the men who conduct it.

"I've only been here eleven years and I'm already batty as hell," says José Perez. "But the best comes out of me when I'm before the kids. What I try to do is make them aware, to look and see what's around them and in them. To wake them up to what's happening on the streets today."

Critics of the Lifers' Group say that young people should not be exposed to men who have committed violent crimes. They point out that scare tactics will not change someone on a destructive course. However, Mike Powers, in charge of counseling at East Jersey State Prison, notes that the program reaches teenagers in a way no other program does. "We have evidence that it has worked for a large number of youths. The fact is that many of these men are very good at what they do."

"A lot of people have jobs they like to do," remarks Willie Allen. That's why they excel at those particular jobs. I think in a lot of our cases we just need to find a notch for ourselves, our little corner in this world and do what we do best. And that's helping kids."

The pride in helping someone affects both the giver and the receiver. Muqtadir Shabazz remembers the first youth he influenced: "I was proud of him, proud of him. Here I am in prison and I reached outside to somebody and helped somebody change his life-style to better himself. Here I am, I committed a crime. And I'm keeping somebody else from doing what I did. In a way it's like giving back the life I once took."

John Stewart finds pride in himself. "I feel good about myself when I stand up on the stage and I talk about the harmfulness of drugs and I know I don't do drugs no more. I do what I preach. It's different when a guy stands up there and says 'don't, don't, don't,' and he's doing, doing, doing. I can hold my head up high and speak heartfelt things because I'm really doing them. I'm giving the kids me. It gives me blessings."

For the Lifers' Group, their program is an oasis in the desert of prison. They cling to it as a shipwrecked man clings to a raft.

"This program is all that my life consists of now," concludes Harvey George. "The first time, I talked about peer pressure and listening to your friends and a kid came up and asked if he could call me. Boy, that was something . . . I see in so many of these kids the same thing I saw in myself as a kid. I always wanted to be older, quicker. When I was fourteen, I wanted to be sixteen. When I got to be sixteen, I couldn't wait

Some members of the Lifers' Group.

until I was eighteen. Then when I got to be eighteen, I wanted to be twenty-one so I could go to the clubs and drink. All of a sudden, now I'm forty some years old and I say what happened? What happened to when I wanted to be eighteen? All my life is gone. I shot my life. And all I got to give is this. To say to kids, you don't have to do this, you don't have to be like me.

"And who would think a prisoner, a guy who messed up

his life, messed up everything he put his hands on, every time he got something good, he screwed it up—and he got a chance to say to somebody, 'you don't have to do that. If you don't believe me, look around you. Look! See. This is where your life is going to end. Do you really want this? Do you want to walk around this place with gray hairs in your head talking about how tough you are? Is that the life you want?' "

BIBLIOGRAPHY

Abbott, Jack Henry. *In the Belly of the Beast: Letters from Prison.* New York: Random House, 1981.

American Correctional Association. *The American Prison: from the Beginning . . . A Pictorial History.* College Park, Maryland: American Correctional Association, 1983.

Berry, Leonard. *Prison: Interviews.* New York: Grossman Publishers, 1972.

Chang, Dae and Armstrong, Warren. *The Prison: Voices from Inside.* Cambridge, Massachusetts: Schenkman Publishing.

Clark, Phyllis Elperin and Lehman, Robert. *Doing Time: A Look at Crime and Prisons.* Hastings House, New York: 1980.

Firestone, Ross. *Getting Busted: Personal Experiences of Arrest, Trial and Prison.* New York: Douglas Books, 1970.

Mitford, Jessica. *Kind and Usual Punishment: The Prison Business.* New York: Knopf, 1973.

Ohlin, Lloyd (editor). *Prisoners in America.* Englewood Cliffs, N.J.: Prentice-Hall, 1973.

INDEX

Richard Wormser has written, produced, and directed more than one hundred films, videotapes, and slide presentations for television, industry, educational institutions, and governmental organizations. His programs have received more than twenty awards.

Among his television credits include: *The Fighting Ministers* (PBS), *Death for a Juvenile?* (the MacNeil-Lehrer Newshour), *The Other Side of Victory* (NEH/PBS), *Up From the Ashes* (3-2-1 Contact), *Joseph* (HBO), *Landscapes of Hope* (PBS), *Other People, Other Places* (ABC).

Richard Wormser is also an author and photographer of books for young adults. Among his more recent works are: *Allan Pinkerton: America's First Private Eye, The Money Book for Children*, and two photographic books on animals.

Mr. Wormser lives in New York City.